This book is a masterpiece! You Are Wanted will captivate your heart, equip you to recover from brokenness, and prepare you to help others. Nicole Langman has poured years of professional training and personal experience into this epic manuscript. She blends therapeutic information, biblical applications, powerful illustrations, and extraordinary take-aways within each chapter. You'll want to purchase one copy for yourself and several more to give to women who need the hope and help this book offers.

–**Carol Kent**, Speaker and Author
He Holds My Hand: Experiencing God's Presence and Protection (Tyndale)

Suffering in the valley of rejection? Hearing all the voices in your head telling you you're not enough and it will always feel like this. Stop right now, buy this book and start reading it immediately! You Are Wanted *leads you out of the pit of rejection so you can reclaim your future. Your good, God appointed future. Written by a therapist who has been where you are, Nicole shares her personal heartbreaks and gifts you with her professional guidance so you can experience freedom from your pain. Chapter by chapter, you will find practical and doable exercises and advice to get your life back.*

–**Robyn Dykstra**, Christian Women's Speaker, Author, Coach

In You Are Wanted, *people who've felt the sting of rejection will find truth to dispel lies, encouragement that diffuses insecurity, and renewed joy to drive away pain from their past. The fact is, we are very much wanted, regardless of what others might have told us. Whether rejection started in childhood, happened in a romantic relationship, came through a friend, or a myriad of other ways our souls can be wounded, it is not a label we must bear until our dying breath. This book will help readers reclaim their lives!*

–**Anita Agers-Brooks**, Business/Life Coach, Common Trauma Expert, and best-selling author of *Getting Through What You Can't Get Over*

Masterfully and vulnerably written, Nicole speaks hope and healing into the hearts of women who have experienced hurt and rejection. Her approach is warm and engaging, presenting biblical truth mingled with real and raw personal experience. She boldly names the places we feel entitled to land and then gently reframes, bringing in the redeeming presence of Jesus, in a way that a new paradigm can be envisioned and embraced. Nicole's many years of experience as a wise, effective therapist are reflected in the practical helps at the end of each chapter. This book is a must-read for every woman who has experienced rejection and for those who are her supporters.

–**Connie Siebert,** Pastor of Care, South Abbotsford Church

This book is a powerful blend of open and honest accounts with rejection, faith-filled truths to dismantle the lies of rejection, and a companion guide to navigate through your personal journey. It's relatable, real, and raw, paired perfectly with wisdom and wit. An approachable, must-read for all people. A journey of hope and healing lies ahead of you in this book. It guides you through the vulnerable path of rejection with such grace, faith-filled wisdom, and practical, ready-to-implement strategies. A comforting read for your soul.

–**Dr. Karen Snow,** Naturopathic Doctor

If you know the pain of rejection, you will find healing and hope in this book. Nicole's tender voice is on every page, pulling together practical truth alongside deeply personal experience. I can hear her smiling, wiping tears and cheering me on as I read, and I'm so grateful. The Christian community needs more voices like this—full of kindness, boots-on-the ground application and sound doctrine.

–**Kathy Slessor,** Director of Integration, Emmanuel Baptist Church

The message of this book is not just advice to others but realities she embodies and practices daily. I have been blown away by her resilience and genuine heart to use her own story to help others experience healing and find purpose. You will be challenged in the best way and truly inspired by her!

—**Kim Moran,** Pastor, Abbotsford, British Columbia

With openness and vulnerability, Nicole leads you through her own journey of dark valleys, pointing you to the Healer of all hurts. Well written and easy to read, this book is full of practical advice. Each chapter ends with key takeaways and thought-provoking questions that help the reader to not only learn from the material but gives them actual steps to take, pivoting toward the healing process. Even if you have not experienced a family breakup you will gain insight and nuggets of truth that you can apply to life's difficult situations!

—**Mary Folkerts,** Writer and Blogger

Personable, funny, and whole-heartedly vulnerable, Nicole will gently lead you through the dark valley of rejection. Using her own experiences as a divorced woman and her skill as a therapist, she exposes all the emotions and pitfalls that seek to ambush you on your journey toward healing. If you find yourself in that valley, the truths in this book will remind you of your identity as a dearly loved daughter of God.

—**Dr. Paul Turner,** Pastor of Worship, Emmanuel Baptist Church Barrie, Ontario

You Are Wanted *is the book you need when rejection tears your life apart and you can't see a path forward through the pieces. As a therapist and fellow sojourner, Nicole helps you discover beauty in the brokenness and hope in the hard places. With personal stories and practical help, this book will be your trusted guide through the Valley of Rejection as you learn to embrace your God-given value.*

—TARYN NERGAARD, Life Coach and Author of *The Reflective Bible Journals*

Nicole's style of writing could best be described as conversational, making a tough subject seem less threatening. Her empathy for others wandering the storm of rejection is clear throughout her work and writing. As I read through Nicole's book, I found that my key feeling was hope—hope in the reminder of my worth in Christ. And the challenging idea of suffering well or my pain having purpose. What powerful and insightful words to help rewrite our narrative!

—JENNIFER C. LEON, MA, RCC - Registered Clinical Counsellor

In You Are Wanted *Nicole reaches deep into her heart and vulnerably shares not only her hurts but also her healing. As a woman who knows the sting of rejection and the healing of Jesus' love for me, I value how Nicole brings us back to the truth of who God says we are, His dying love for us, and the hope and promise we find there. This is a book I will always keep multiple copies of, and confidently use as a resource and support, not only personally, but to the women I help in my life coaching. It is a timely and invaluable book that reminds us there is purpose and promise in the pain.*

—JANICE STONE, Professional Certified Life Coach and founder of Janice Stone Life Coach

The open, gaping wound of rejection, of being unwanted by a spouse needs the Christ-centered salve that this book offers. Written from a woman's perspective, there isn't another book on the market that blends personal, raw experiences with concrete, biblically-based, therapeutic steps to help people heal. While it's been many years since I experienced this firsthand, I found myself wishing I had had this resource then, and even found myself finally identifying pivot points in my own life.

–**JACKIE GLENDENNING,** Fellow Rejection Survivor

This book speaks truth into dark places, and is a poignant work reminding you who you are and WHOSE you are. Nicole's vulnerability, sensibility and compassion in relaying her personal experiences of the unthinkables is intriguing and life giving. She shows how the un-thinkables (abandonment, rejection, heartbreak, feeling unchosen, and the rubble and mess of life) are turned around by the TRUTH of the Living Word. God has the final say in your life, giving you HOPE and an identity apart from how others define you. Your value and worth are defined by the power of Jesus.

–**CORINA KROP,** Teacher, Abbotsford, British Columbia

Rejection in one form or another is the common lot of the human experience and none of us escape the damage. This book offers compassionate and concrete help from someone who's been there. Nicole will begin to feel like a friend who is beside you as you walk through YOUR rescue story.

–**DEBBIE BEST,** Small Group Leader, Chilliwack, British Columbia

You Are Wanted

RECLAIMING THE TRUTH
OF WHO YOU ARE

Nicole Langman

You Are Wanted: Reclaiming the Truth of Who You Are

Brookstone Publishing Group
100 Missionary Ridge
Birmingham, AL 35242

Copyright © 2021 by Nicole Langman

No part of this publication may be reproduced, stored in a retrieval system, or transmitted in any form or by any means—electronic, mechanical, photocopying, recording, or otherwise—without the prior written permission of the publisher.

Brookstone Publishing Group serves its authors as they express their views, which may not express the views of the publisher.

All Scripture quotations, unless otherwise indicated, are taken from THE HOLY BIBLE, NEW INTERNATIONAL VERSION® NIV®
Copyright © 1973, 1978, 1984 by International Bible Society®
Used by permission. All rights reserved worldwide.

Scriptures marked ESV are taken from The Holy Bible, English Standard Version® (ESV®), Copyright© 2001 by Crossway, a publishing ministry of Good News Publishers. Used by permission. All rights reserved.

Scripture quotations marked (NLT) are taken from the Holy Bible, New Living Translation, copyright © 1996, 2004, 2007, 2013, 2015 by Tyndale House Foundation. Used by permission of Tyndale House Publishers, Inc., Carol Stream, Illinois 60188. All rights reserved.

ISBN: 978-1-949856-58-3 paperback
ISBN: 978-1-56309-555-9 ebook

1 2 3 4 5—25 24 23 22 21

Printed in the United States of America

To Brent,

you are God's exclamation point in His love letter to me.

About the Cover

Kintsukuroi is the Japanese art of repairing broken pottery with gold, emphasizing the beauty of the breaks. It is believed that the repaired pottery is especially beautiful, not in spite of its scars, but because of them. When we hold our wounds and our brokenness up to Jesus, as this woman on the cover is doing, we find He is the Perfect Potter, and brings beauty from the broken places.

Contents

Introduction		1
How to Read this Book		11
Part 1	The R Word that Hurts	17
Chapter 1	The Problem of Rejection	19
Chapter 2	Rejection Recovery Process	31
Chapter 3	The Co-Accusers	43
Chapter 4	War Wounds and Battle Scars	57
Chapter 5	Rejection is a Liar	71
Part 2	The R Words that Heal	81
Chapter 6	Relished	83
Chapter 7	Rescued	95
Chapter 8	Redeemed	105
Chapter 9	Released	115
Chapter 10	Remember	129
Part 3	Reclaiming Your True Identity	139
Chapter 11	An Identity of Free	141
Chapter 12	An Identity of Overcomer	153
Chapter 13	An Identity of Courage	165
Chapter 14	An Identity of Wanted & Chosen	177
Chapter 15	The Problem of Staying Stuck	189

Part 4	Roadblocks and Reminders		201
	Chapter 16	The Temptation of Revenge	203
	Chapter 17	Forgiveness: The Chapter I'm Scared to Write	217
	Chapter 18	Grieving the Loss of the Living	231
	Chapter 19	For the Momma's Heart	243
	Chapter 20	Your Story: A Survival Guide for Another Woman's Soul	255

Some Final Thoughts	269
Scriptures to Ease Anxiety and Bring Comfort	273
Acknowledgments	277
About the Author	279
Notes	281

Introduction

"I am not what happened to me; I am what I choose to become."

—CARL GUSTAV JUNG

While sand spilled through my toes, and the sun crept up over a perfect beach in Mexico, I noticed a shift in my pain. I hoped this mother-daughter vacation would be a healing ointment on my broken heart after a devastating and overwhelming year.

Wrestling with God through the dark valley of rejection and judging myself for the wrestle had become my new pastimes. *Why did this continue to hurt so much? What was wrong with me that I was still feeling so broken?* It had been almost eight months since my husband of nearly twenty years decided to leave our family. No, it was seven months, twenty-two days, and a handful of hours that took my breath away, not that I was counting

The rejection story was like an untamed, angry beast in my mind, running loose with belittling statements and criticism that felt like a punch in the gut on a good day. And had me totally wrecked, face down on the floor on the bad days. I had been catapulted into a deep valley, faceplanted hard on the valley floor, and I was finding it hard to breathe.

Our current culture says losing one's spouse to death is something bad that happens *to you*, while losing your spouse to divorce is something bad that happens *because of you*. I was in this latter group, the so-called faulty group of people who lose their spouse because of some intolerable inadequacy, bad behaviour, or shortcoming.

In my case, to add insult to injury, I was facing the shame of losing two marriages. Circumstances outside of my control left me, in both cases, grappling with the heartache of loss, and rebuilding a new identity and a new life.

If I allowed myself to be honest, I was beginning to believe the tyrannical rejection story in my mind. Maybe I really was unlovable, unwanted, and undeserving of happiness. Rejection was having a heyday in my mind. And the shame, anxiety, grief, and anger that accompanied it were monsters I didn't feel equipped to handle. I wrestled hard, and I grieved deeply.

So, with my Bible open to the Psalms, I tilted my face to the sky, and in my very innermost being, I begged, maybe even challenged God to explain Himself. I don't know about you, but when I wrestle with God, some of it happens in my heart, and some of it gets spoken out loud. On this day in Mexico, alone on this perfect beach, I cried out to Him, declaring my anger and hurt, begging Him to reveal His reasons and plans.

In desperation, I heard myself say, *Go ahead then, take it all. You've already taken everything anyway.* In retrospect, this challenge sounds more like a temper-tantrum than a prayer. But in a grace-filled, peace-wrapped love message straight from my Heavenly Father's heart came these words, *I've left you with the best parts. Trust me with what's left.*

Startled by this almost audible message, I quickly lifted my head and looked around. To my left was an incredible display of brilliant colours. Windswept clouds seemed to collect the purple and orange hues casting glowing rays of light onto the water, dancing and shining as though on a stage. A perfect backdrop, the blue sky provided the ultimate canvas for this early morning reminder—fresh starts are beautiful.

Mesmerized by this scene, it seemed to change and shine more brilliantly by the second. With my face tilted to the sun, content to just sit and enjoy every perfect sunlit moment, I became aware that for the first time in many months, I could feel my soul find rest. More gentle prompting, and with a nudge from Heaven, my attention was drawn to the right.

Almost mirroring the storm in my heart, heavy rain was pounding the shores of the resorts not too far in the distance. The sky was not only dark, it was fierce, and the lightning in the distance seemed to put exclamation marks all over this menacing scene. I looked quickly to my left, noticing the sunrise still in progress. And then a glance to my right, I observed the storm raging with all the anger it could muster.

In a second, my heart knew this message—beauty and heartache can co-exist. Fresh starts and beautiful new things are possible, even when storms are pounding the shores.

Focusing solely on the storm causes us to miss the beauty of the sunrise. Remaining strictly attentive to the heaviness, pain, and loss in life will result in a singular perspective, becoming the primary viewpoint from which we view our life. What we focus on becomes our truth.

The rejection we've experienced is true and the losses are real. The heaviness and pain, legitimate. But when we lock eyes with that storm, our attention remains consumed by it. The storm is real, but it's not the only thing that's real. Rejection can hold pain *and* promise at the same time.

> Rejection can hold pain *and* promise at the same time.

The pain of the faceplant on the valley floor is not as fresh today as it was on that day in Mexico. But my heart remembers well, and my soul bears those unique rejection scars so common to many of us.

Pivot Points

I never wanted to be a rejection researcher. But when everything I thought was true about my marriage slammed up against my new reality, it left me face down in the deepest valley of my life.

I call this valley the Valley of Rejection. It's not a place any of us want to visit and it was certainly not a place I thought I would end up. But there I was, heart-wrecked in the darkest season of my life.

Heartbreak and trauma are the ultimate pivot points, aren't they? A radical repositioning can screech to a halt the former and familiar, thrusting us into the new. Some pivots in life are welcome and pleasant, bringing wonderful shifts in our lives.

But that's not what has happened for you and me, is it?

You and I know not all pivots are pleasant. Being hurled from one identity into another brings an onslaught of injuries. Rejection is a deep soul wound and a vicious assault on truth. In its wake, it leaves a throbbing heartache requiring gentleness, self-compassion and active self-care.

If no one has given you permission yet, can I just be the first to tell you—be extra kind to yourself. Active self-care in the midst of this valley is crucial for healing. Self-compassion and kindness are essential when brokenness comes calling.

My daughter and I took this concept quite seriously. One particularly challenging day for us, we found ourselves booking pedicures and scrolling travel websites. It didn't take too much convincing—her birthday was approaching and that provided the perfect excuse to secure a week-long getaway in Mexico. It was my hope that this week away together would soothe some of the sore spots, and help breathe healing into our next season. I could not have predicted the significance of this trip. The pivot came on day three, when I embraced the message of the sunrise and the storm.

Beauty and heartache can co-exist. In our pain, let's keep a keen eye out for the reminders from Heaven that God is still at work. He has not left us to navigate this storm alone.

The Truth and the Lies

I absolutely must start this whole thing with one crucial message. It's a message I desperately needed to hear during a particularly awful time in my life, and it's a message I want you to hear too. I want you to hear it with your heart. I want you to know this with your soul. If I could, I would hold your beautiful, God-designed face in my hands, look you in the eyes, and declare these very important, truer than true words—YOU, MY FRIEND, ARE WANTED.

Not just a little bit wanted, but you are wholeheartedly, shake the heavens, and move mountains wanted.

You are chosen. You are delighted in, and you are adored.

My heart's desire for you is that you would let those words, those truths, saturate your soul. And through that deep knowing, you would understand your worth and your desirability in a new way.

You are wanted.

I don't know exactly what brings you to the pages of this book, but I know your heart is sore. Probably more than sore actually. If your heart is in the shape mine was a few years ago, it feels like it's been ripped out of you, sent through a blender, and handed back to you in pieces.

I see you. And I know this brokenheartedness.

The unthinkable has happened. It feels like a slow-moving nightmare, full of awfulness that takes your breath away. The sharp edges of grief are overwhelming and, as you put one brave foot in front of the other, confusion and pain tag-team you through each moment.

> Rejection catapults us into a devastating spin-cycle of heartache, leaving us questioning what we thought was real, and pointing at us the gnarled finger of shame.

I get this unthinkable nightmare. Rejection catapults us into a devastating spin-cycle of heartache, leaving us questioning what we thought was real, and pointing at us the gnarled finger of shame. Grief is thick and the heartbreak is sometimes more than you can bear.

This is not how you wanted things to go.

The truth is you're reading this book because someone you love has walked away. This walking away may be physical, but since rejection happens on many levels you may find yourself feeling emotionally, sexually or spiritually abandoned long before someone leaves physically. In every case, the walking away screamed a terrible message to you that sunk deep into your core:

- I am unwanted
- I am rejectable
- I am unlovable
- I am inadequate
- I am ugly
- I am replaceable

- I am incapable of _____
- I will never be _____
- I am _____

My heart is heavy as I write these words. I know the pain of feeling unwanted, of feeling unchosen. I understand the make-you-crazy-ness and confusion of the unravelling. And I, too, have heard the horrible words and felt the deep anguish of loss. The walking away left me broken and desperate for healing, and it had me wondering if in fact, I really was rejectable.

I wrestled hard with this wondering. My journal from those early days speaks of a desperate cry for clarity and understanding—begging God for answers.

Through the rubble and the mess came a message right from our Heavenly Father's heart. The message stopped me in my tracks, and in many ways lifted me out of the quicksand of wondering.

If you can, open your Bible to Zephaniah 3:17 and let your heart hear these words, "For the LORD YOUR GOD is LIVING among you. He is a MIGHTY SAVIOR. He will TAKE DELIGHT in you with GLADNESS. With HIS LOVE He will CALM ALL YOUR FEARS. He will REJOICE OVER YOU WITH JOYFUL SONGS" (emphasis is mine, NLT).

The Lord your God—your Saviour—delights in you. His love is so great that it calms your fears. He is celebrating you. The Creator of the World is singing over you.

You are highly valued, deeply loved, and grandly celebrated. While it is true that someone has walked away it is not true that you are rejectable, because God declares you chosen and fully accepted. And it is not true that you are unwanted, because the King of Kings wanted you so desperately that He died a brutal death just to have you back.

> But when we measure our value by the acceptance or rejection of another person, we get a deeply inaccurate picture of our worth.

This might be a bit confusing, I admit, I struggled too. But when we measure our value by the acceptance or rejection of another person, we get a deeply inaccurate picture of our worth. God gets the final say about our value. And He declares us wanted.

Rejection doesn't want you to remember this truth. Its sinister message stands in stark contrast with the truth God says about you. Naturally the rejection hurts, but can I be honest? It's the story it generates in our hearts, and the lies it feeds us about ourselves that hurts the most.

And that's why I wrote this book. The rejection that rocked my world fed me lies I began to believe and dragged me away from the truth of who I was.

So, while this book is about rejection, it's mostly about hope.

It's a book about identity. It's a book about healing from the unthinkable, and reclaiming who you are. And it's a bold walk away from the lies of rejection, toward this very important truth:

You are wanted. You are chosen.

While you have been through the unthinkable and picked up this book because rejection is a real and recent trauma, you will find in these pages a reclaiming of the truth.

You are wanted.

Navigating the Valley

My heart feels heavy as I write this, knowing that the woman who holds this book is facing heartbreak and heavy loss. I am so sorry that you are in a place that brings you to the pages of this book. The journey that brought you here has been awful, and I grieve with you.

You must be a person of great hope and tremendous courage, plodding through the devastation of rejection. As a woman who knows this pain, I see you, and I stand with you in this storm.

You're in a valley right now. Maybe you've just arrived here on the heels of a blindside, surprise heartbreak, or disappointment. Or maybe you have been in this valley a long time where rejection is familiar to you, and you expect the pain to continue. Whatever situation led you here, this place of rejection is dark, and you are exhausted from carrying the weight of it.

This may seem unimaginable to you right now, but I believe in my soul you are on the cusp of something beautiful. Your days are known by our loving Heavenly Father. He sees you and this valley you're in right now. And He knows your pain—the rejection story weighing you down.

Rejection is a reality for us both. And while I don't know your story, I do understand your pain. With certainty I can say, while you have been rejected, you are absolutely not rejectable.

> Your worth and acceptability does not rest on the opinion of any human being.

Your worth and acceptability does not rest on the opinion of any human being. You are deeply loved and completely acceptable because Jesus says you are. On these pages you will find the true stories of women like us—women who have felt the heartbreak of rejection, and who have found their identity and healing through a deeper understanding of Jesus.

Please read this book knowing that the woman writing these words believes you will get through your valley and stand victorious on the other side. My hope is that the following valley-to-victory stories, along with the therapeutic strategies on these pages, will act as a supportive embrace. I pray you put one trusting foot in front of the other through this difficult season of your life.

The grief is heavy, and the loss is real. And while it may be hard to believe, within the grief and the loss lies beauty. How do I know this? Because I know the heart of our Heavenly Father, and He wraps the most precious gifts in the most unlikely packages. We can trust Him with what's left. Let's lean hard on Him as we navigate this valley together.

Love,
Nicole

How to Read this Book

What Is Narrative Therapy?

I want to introduce you to narrative therapy. When you get into the swing of this approach to problem management, you will find it helps in other areas of your life as well. The women I work with absolutely love these strategies.

Please understand that this is not an exhaustive representation of narrative therapy, but for the purpose of this book there are two key concepts I want you to keep in mind:

1. Narrative therapy externalizes (even personifies) the problem.

I see your raised eyebrows. Trust me when I tell you this—externalizing the problem will liberate you from it. When we externalize, we separate, and this offers the opportunity to interact with the problem differently.

You will hear narrative therapists say, "You're not the problem, the problem is the problem. We need to change your relationship to the problem."

When we view the problem as something outside of us, we gain distance from it. This distancing strategy helps us view the problem differently and change our relationship to it. And when we do that, we feel empowered to walk away from its lies.

Children are fantastic at this externalizing and personifying practise. When I worked with children many years ago, I found the primary issue they brought to counseling was the problem of fear.

I remember one little guy in particular who battled bedtime fear. I asked my little friend to describe the problem, and he told me these magic words, "It's there every night, and it makes going to bed in my new sheets no fun. And I hate it, but it just keeps being there." Johnny was a budding narrative therapist and didn't even know it yet.

Among others, I asked him these narrative questions:

1. Johnny, what does bedtime fear take from you that you would like back?

2. What happens to bedtime fear when the lights come on? And what does this say about its power?

3. What does bedtime fear not know about you that it might be surprised about?

4. If your Mom or Dad could talk to bedtime fear, what would they say?

5. What is there in you Johnny, that can help you stand up to bedtime fear and send it packing?

Johnny was a champ at this! He navigated his way through several different externalizing questions resulting in a newfound determination to not give in to bedtime fear when it tried to steal his fun. He recognized its weakness, and He recognized his own strength. He changed his relationship to the problem, and stood up to it.

That's the process of externalizing and personifying. You will find throughout these pages I speak about rejection, anxiety, shame and other problems as external to us. It's an essential aspect of this therapeutic approach, and will empower you to take power back from the problem.

2. *Narrative therapy seeks to help us create a new story about ourselves and our lives.*

We call this practice re-authoring, or re-storying. Life hands us all kinds of experiences and events—some very good, and some very bad. How we interpret and understand these experiences and events greatly impacts our lives. The meaning we attach to them becomes the story we believe about ourselves.

The Stories We Hold

We carry many different stories about ourselves at the same time. For example, you may hold a story of competence about how you do your work while at the same time hold a story of inadequacy as a parent. Though we carry many stories, there is usually one that's dominant.

Your dominant story will inform all the other areas of your life. So, if that dominant story becomes: *I am unwanted*, it creates a ripple effect and permeates other stories.

So, take for example the problem of rejection. When we have an experience with rejection, we develop a story about ourselves.

For me, the rejection story went like this: *Nicole, you would be able to keep your husband if you were more attractive. You're just a really difficult person. You are not worthy of being loved for who you are, and you cannot keep a man because you are unlovable. He's right, you're too much.*

In my mind, this was a dominant story about inadequacy and undeservedness.

And on the heels of that message, came this message: *You should have done more. You should have been better. You should have been prettier, funnier, smarter, whatever-er . . . just not you. He's right, you're not enough.*

The 'shoulds' were relentless and fed a shame story as long as my arm.

Okay, now it's your turn. What is the rejection story spinning in your heart? What does it have you believing about yourself?

_____

_____

_____

We will aggressively challenge that rejection story in this book. It's not true of you and it's time for it to go.

It's my prayer that the rejection story you carry would be re-storied, and you would embrace a hope-filled narrative, focused on your strengths and all that makes you beautiful.

Rejection Recovery Section

At the end of each chapter is a section entitled "Rejection Recovery." It includes:

- A scripture verse
- Four therapeutic questions or activities
- A journal prompt
- A guided prayer

I encourage you to spend time after each chapter working through the Rejection Recovery section as a way to support your healing. Writing things down imbeds the learning deeper into our brains, and that will make for quicker recall when you need it.

You will notice I use three different versions of the Bible throughout this book. The New International Version (NIV), The New Living Translation (NLT), and The English Standard Version (ESV). Don't be afraid to make notes in your Bible and underline scriptures that jump out to you. This will act as a quick reference for you when you reflect back on this time in your life.

Okay, I think it's time to get started. What an honour to journey with you through this season of your life.

Let's go!

PART 1

The R Word that Hurts

CHAPTER 1

The Problem of Rejection

"The real difficulty is to overcome how you think about yourself."

—Maya Angelou

"Can I stay here forever?" I begged from my asylum under her desk. Mrs. Dixon had graciously provided me shelter in her classroom, and my 13-year-old heart was in desperate need of her nurturing kindness to me.

"You can stay here for now," came the gentle voice from above.

Things had not at all gone as planned on this fateful day. Our school was raising money for Easter Seals, and we were in tight competition with another elementary school in our area. As the student council president, I made the cataclysmic decision to invite the sixth graders to the Easter fundraising dance. As important rights of passage, these dances were precious and reserved for the seventh and eighth graders. While inviting the younger group of students may have increased our chances of winning the competition, it was still out of the question. We were generous, but not *invite-sixth-graders* generous and my knee-jerk decision landed hard among my peers.

What ensued was an eighth-grade mutiny. To my horror, my closest friends circulated a petition and collected support to not only have me thrown out of leadership, but to ultimately leave me friendless if I didn't resign my position and uninvite the sixth graders.

I remember the moment this petition was slid forcefully across my desk by the hand of a close friend. There were four columns, requiring my peers to write out their names in the first column, and then check the column that best reflected their position: *Invite the Sixth Graders* or *Don't Invite Them*. And then the final column, *I won't be friends with Nicole if Grade Six comes to the dance.*

I can still see the folded arms and coy smiles on the faces of the girls I thought were my friends as they waited for my reaction to their protest. With all of the courage I could muster, I stood up from my desk, and went where every thirteen-year-old girl goes when her friends hold a mutiny—the bathroom. If you've been on the receiving end of bullying, you know that the school bathroom is not a private place to have a good cry. They were right on my heels, those angry, so-called friends of mine.

Very quickly, I decided I needed a safer space to express my feelings. With startling emotion, I burst out of the stall, and ran past them to Mrs. Dixon's room. Dropping to the floor and crawling under her desk seemed a bit dramatic, but she was unphased as she moved her knees to the side, offering safe passage.

There I was, as small as I could get, knees to chest in the safest place I could find. My snotty nose, tear-soaked face pressed up against Mrs. Dixon's pantyhose.

This was my first real experience with rejection. The petition showed that about half of my friends would be willing to break up with me if the sixth graders came to the fundraising dance. While I was angry, I was also scared. And if I'm honest, I was totally shocked and completely blindsided.

That's the thing about rejection, isn't it? We go about our business when just like that, the person we love walks away, the job we worked hard for is over, the friend we believed would be there

> Our deepest need is for connection and belonging

forever is gone. The blindside of rejection creates a ripple effect of pain that seeps into our souls. Our deepest need is for connection and belonging—we were created for it—but when rejection shows up it rips away our sense of belonging, and robs us of connection, leaving us to wrestle with our worth.

That's what I was doing under the desk tucked up beside Mrs. Dixon. I was wrestling with my worth. I rattled off a number of potential options, frantic for her feedback, willing to do whatever she suggested. I was ready to quit, and I was ready to call off the whole dance just to make this go away. Anxiety was running amuck, and I was bartering with myself, weighing my options against my thirteen-year-old convictions. Her words that day were like salve on my heart and still hold true today.

In her perfect teacher way, this wise woman said confidently, "This will pass. Don't let this keep you from doing the right thing or being who you are."

I did eventually crawl out from under Mrs. Dixon's desk and face my peers. The sixth graders did come to the dance, helping us raise a lot of money for Easter Seals, securing the win and allowing us to present a fairly impressive cheque on their televised program that year. And Mrs. Dixon was right, the pain did pass, and so did the discomfort of the situation.

Hustle, Harm, and Healing

This early experience with rejection taught me painful but important lessons. By its very nature, rejection drives us to hustle for our worth, to hustle for evidence that we are wanted. This hustle may happen in our hearts at first, but in many cases, it eventually drives behaviours that can become harmful. In the hustle we may find ourselves striving toward acceptance outside of God's will. Rejection can be so destabilizing that in an effort to disprove the messages of rejection, we engage in behaviours that hurt us and move us further away from the path we are created for.

Rejection can drive the best of us toward harmful choices. If you're like me and have felt the devastating sting of spousal rejection, the struggle with worthiness can lead to choices and behaviours that hurt us even more deeply than the rejection itself. Some of the post-rejection coping strategies reported to me in counseling are: over-eating, excessive drinking, returning to harmful historical habits that were left behind, and building new, not-so-healthy relationships.

Full disclosure—the early days in the valley of rejection were especially dark for me. The words my husband had said to me ran like wildebeests in my mind, creating a breeding ground for insecurity and self-deprecation. I felt ugly. I felt unwanted. And I was desperate for someone to say none of that was true. In my vulnerability I joined a dating site. I'm not proud of this. It had only been about five months since my marriage ended and I was in no way ready to consider another relationship. But I went ahead and joined anyway.

This short-lived experiment certainly offered a distraction from the pain, and the temporary ego boost provided moments of respite. But the online admiration from strangers was superficial and an ineffective solution to a heart problem that no human could heal. I needed Jesus. I needed to remain focused on what He says about me, and His unfathomable love needed to be my primary source of comfort.

While rejection misleads us toward temporary, superficial fixes, the truth is that none of these provide the healing we find when

> While rejection misleads us toward temporary, superficial fixes, the truth is that none of these provide the healing we find when we run to the always open arms of Jesus.

we run to the always open arms of Jesus.

When someone doesn't choose us, we risk making them the authority on our value. It's as though they somehow represent all of humanity and have the us-given power to determine our worthiness. Signing up for that dating app was an impulsive quick fix rooted in the fear that perhaps my husband was right. Perhaps what he said was true of me. But while I had been rejected by one person, it did not reflect the opinion of the masses, nor did it in any way represent the opinion of my Heavenly Father.

This aha moment led me to a life changing shift in focus. Rejection sends us on a scavenger hunt to collect evidence that we are not what has been said of us. This hustle leads to bad choices and further hurt. When we tilt our heads to lock eyes with the One Who knows us best and loves us most, the scavenger hunt becomes unnecessary and the hustle is replaced with peace.

Closing the dating app a few days after signing up was an act of rebellion against the tactics of rejection. Chasing after numbing strategies that only temporarily ease the pain of rejection, ultimately leads us down a path of destruction and away from the heart of our Heavenly Father.

God does not allow purpose-less suffering. Our pain holds promise and learning how to lean into the discomfort rather than run from it, will always lead us toward the healing hands of Jesus. He has the answers, and He will not turn us away regardless of the destructive choices we may have explored while in this difficult valley.

Humanhood and Rejection Navigation

Humanhood means you have experienced rejection. It may have crept into your life at a young age when a parent or loved one walked away. Or perhaps your rejection story starts in grade school when friends turned their backs on you. Maybe you didn't make the team, or you've been uninvited, left out, forgotten, or let go. Adulthood doesn't get easier, does it? If you got through your youth without facing rejection, being an adult provides lots of time to make up for that. Job loss, relationship breakdowns, and marital infidelity wreak havoc on us and thicken the rejection story.

I work with women in my practice on a regular basis who have faced the very painful experience of having a parent walk away or show little interest in them. And for many, their partner has changed his mind about the relationship and decided to leave. Maybe your child has alienated themselves from you by their own doing, or the influence of another person. And perhaps you have a longstanding, percolating feeling of not fitting in, of not being accepted.

Rejection is a human experience. We all will face rejection at some point or another, and that unfortunately, is very real and very true. What isn't true though, is that you are rejectable. Your very existence was thought out, planned, and orchestrated by the Creator of the World. He made you. He chose you. And He celebrates you. You are favored by the King of Kings. This truth means that you are absolutely not rejectable.

As you read this book, keep in mind three important things about rejection:

1. Rejection creates a confirmation bias. This bias is a tendency to look for, interpret, and recall information that confirms or supports our philosophy or opinion about

something. When we believe we are rejectable, we notice rejections and even rewrite history in our minds to confirm our rejectability. All of this builds the victim story in our hearts and keeps us from seeing the counter-story, the narrative that says we are loved, celebrated, and chosen.

2. Rejection collects more rejection and assumes intentions of others. When we accept the story that we are rejectable, it can cause us to project this rejection story about ourselves onto those around us. This may start out as a defense mechanism, but ends with additional rejections, thus feeding the 'rejectable' philosophy we're carrying. Believing we are rejectable will make us small, insecure, and anxious. And when we go into the world already believing we are going to be rejected, owning a story that we are inadequate, we actually set ourselves up for further rejection.

3. Our brains respond as though we have been physically injured. This is why rejection hurts more than we think it will. A few years ago, scientists studying rejection placed people in MRI machines and asked them to recall recent experiences with rejection. Amazingly, the areas of the brain that were activated during this experiment are the same areas activated during experiences with physical pain. Even small rejections evoke serious emotional pain.

This isn't likely to surprise you, but we tend to be able to recall the pain of rejection easier than physical pain. This means our brains remember emotional pain easier than physical pain. While we know something hurts physically, we forget how that pain felt after a period of time. With emotional pain, especially rejection, we remember how it felt. That said, this doesn't mean the rejection you're facing will always feel like this. No, it just means that when asked, we are able to recall how this pain feels easier than physical pain.

The rejection narrative is debilitating. And while rejection itself hurts, the story it tells us and the lies we believe about ourselves bring the greatest injuries. We may not have control over the rejection, but we do have control over the stories spinning through our minds and hearts. Let's challenge the rejection story, and decide on a new narrative. A truth narrative. This journey out of the valley begins with a choice. Will you agree with the rejection story, or turn your focus toward recovery and the One calling you through?

KEY TAKEAWAYS

- You're not the problem, the problem is the problem.

- Rejection does not have the authority to measure your worth.

- When someone doesn't choose us, we risk making them the authority on our value. It's as though they somehow represent all of humanity and have the us-given power to determine our worthiness.

- Rejection can drive you toward harmful choices.

- While rejection hurts, it's the resulting messages you tell yourself that hurt the most.

- Your pain holds purpose.

- While you may have experienced rejection, you are not rejectable to God.

- You are fully accepted, loved, and celebrated by Jesus.

Luke 15:7

REJECTION RECOVERY

> So be strong and courageous! Do not be afraid and do not panic before them. For the LORD your God will personally go ahead of you. He will neither fail you nor abandon you (Deuteronomy 31:6 NLT).

THERAPEUTIC QUESTIONS

- What does rejection have you thinking about yourself?
- If you could challenge the story of rejection in your heart, where and how would you challenge it?
- What time of day is the rejection story strongest? Why do you think rejection chooses this time to trouble you?
- What is one bold thing you can do to stand up to rejection when it tries to drag you down a path not meant for you?

JOURNAL PROMPT

What does life without the rejection story look like? How will I feel when this has healed?

Jesus, thank you for travelling this valley with me. Rejection is so painful, and this journey is overwhelming. I feel desperate for reminders of my worth. Please come close to me and breathe Your words of truth into my broken heart. Help me to keep my eyes locked on You and not on the story of rejection. I know you are with me through this, please give me the courage to lean on You through it all. Amen.

CHAPTER 2

Rejection Recovery Process

"There are far, far better things ahead than any we leave behind."

—C.S. Lewis

It was 4:30 in the morning on a Tuesday, and until this particular day I had been up to my knees in the quicksand of the valley of rejection. The pain of the rejection was emotionally debilitating, and while I looked like a woman who had it together on the outside, on the inside I was wrecked. Days felt like years, weekends were the enemy—highlighting my aloneness. It was a moment-by-moment struggle.

Mornings marked the start of another day away from the life I had known and loved. Unwelcome messengers, mornings pointed a condemning finger at my flaws. They reminded me I was unwanted. Unchosen.

But on this particular day, I awoke with a deep knowing in my heart unlike anything I had experienced before. This knowing had me leaping out of bed and dancing in my living room.

The ears of my heart heard these words: *Nicole, I adore you. I choose you. Will you trust me?*

The King of Kings had heard my distress call, dropped everything, and came running to my little apartment where He found me wrestling with my heartbreak. His love prompted Him to action, and He was asking me to choose.

Link arms with the Creator of the Universe, or go it alone? I could choose to think on His Truth about me, or I could choose to spin on the things another flawed human had said and done.

Choosing to move forward was an act of trust and obedience. It was me saying *yes* to God. That's it.

> Recovery starts with a choice to trust God and engage in a recovery process *with* Him.

Recovery starts with a choice to trust God and engage in a recovery process *with* Him. But I need to be honest, the choice to recover does not mean we experience freedom right away. It simply means we are locking eyes with Jesus and allowing Him to guide us toward wholeness—away from brokenness. The choice means we are willing to stand up to the nasty narrative that has us whirling about the loss and focused on our inadequacies. The choice means we are going to shun the rejection-based messages and cling to God's words about us. The choice is where we put a cog in the spinning wheels of pain-based thinking and declare a new direction.

Our yes to God marks the pivot point that moves us away from the pain and toward the purpose God has for us.

My 4:30 a.m. pivot point came with a verse from Isaiah. If you can, grab your Bible and have a good look at this verse. It says, *"When you go through deep waters, I will be with you. When you go through rivers of difficulty, you will not drown. When you walk through the fire of oppression, you will not be burned up; the flames will not consume you"* (Isaiah 43:2 NLT).

Notice how God reminds us here that we are not alone? He does not say He will keep us from trouble—His promise is to travel with us. When He says He is with us, we can trust Him. When He promises to bring us through, He absolutely will. This is a movement-based passage, full of promises and packed with hope. God is purposeful in His actions. He does not haphazardly check in on us, giving us the nod from time to time. No, He takes this process seriously, and is fully invested in our recovery. Why? Because like a loving parent, God wants us to understand our value, His unfathomable love and His absolute acceptance of us.

Building Bounce-back

But humanhood offers human interactions, and countless up close, painfully personal encounters with rejection. It happens at a micro-level daily, when we find ourselves not included in that coffee date, or when our friends don't like our posts on Instagram. And it happens in big ways when our partners or close friends walk away, a parent or child chooses to not be in relationship with us, or when we work hard for something we don't get. Rejection and the fear of rejection inform so much of what we do, how we live, and who we are, that it's fair to say it's one of the greatest influencers of our time.

Since rejection is so common, developing rejection resilience is necessary for healing. Rejection resilience involves establishing a truth-based philosophy about ourselves and developing an internal boundary system to screen out conflicting messages.

The rejection resilience process isn't about avoiding pain. That's not humanly possible. Rather, it seeks to build a firm foundation based on Truth—reducing our sensitivity to rejection. An important aspect of this book is developing a truth-based philosophy about yourself. It seeks to help you own your story and travel this difficult season of your life in a way that honours you and your unique situation.

One day you will find yourself on the other side of the valley, the sun will shine again, rejection will be a distant memory, the pain will be gone. What do you want to be able to say about how you moved through this season? How do you want to feel about yourself on the other side? This is about honouring your older self—the person who traveled well.

> We cannot be a victim and a victor at the same time.

We cannot be a victim and a victor at the same time. We must choose. The victim mentality is problem-focused, staring up at rejection, taking orders from it and accepting the narrative it spews. On the other hand, the victor mindset stands tall, notices the rejection but turns boldly away from it and embraces a healing narrative—focused on recovery.

Has there been an injustice? Quite likely. Have you been mistreated, misunderstood, misrepresented? Yes. While these are true, you can choose who you are going to be in this. While rejection tempts you to focus on the injustice and pain, you have a responsibility to yourself and your Heavenly Father to put down the victim flag. This courageous decision is an essential first step and your pivot point in this recovery journey. It makes room for you to pick up the flag of victory, turn toward freedom, and begin your homecoming trek through to the other side.

Rejection Recovery

So, what is Rejection Recovery? Simply, it's a process requiring an intentional shift in focus and a deliberate move toward healing. The five key elements of this process are below, and while they are not necessarily in order, you will feel yourself move through them. When you find yourself helping others through their pain or finding forgiveness for the person who has hurt you, allow yourself a moment to celebrate. This is an important indicator you are moving toward healing.

- Regaining self confidence
- Finding hope
- Exploring the learning and embracing a new identity
- Working toward forgiveness
- Helping others (helping here is defined as offering supportive, loving encouragement)

To this end, it helps to have a look at the stages of recovery. Many of us bounce back and forth in these stages. No two people travel this process the same way, and each stage takes time to work through. Resist the urge to judge yourself if one day you feel liberated in the Recovery Stage, and the next day you wake up with a backslide into the Wrestle. Have patience and grace with yourself—and with the process. It will get easier.

Stages of Rejection Recovery

Stage 1 - Shock - Rejection almost always brings with it a level of shock. Lasting for mere moments or for many months, shock leaves us in disbelief. This is the nosedive stage, and it can literally take our breath away. We may find that this stage can cause us to feel desperate, potentially leading us into an emotional and mental scramble, to make sense of what has just happened.

We are likely to play and replay the rejection story in our minds. We talk about it constantly. trying to make some sense out of the situation. It's all-consuming and overwhelming and if you're in this stage—please hold on tight to this—it will not always feel like this. You will not feel like this forever. And your Heavenly Father is standing close by, calling you forward.

The shock stage introduces three problems:

We are infested with a nasty narrative. The influx of self-condemning messages on the heels of the heartbreak leaves us walking wounded through this pain-filled season.

We experience disbelief and panic. This blindsides us, creating a ripple effect that increases anxiety and confusion. In an effort to make sense of the rejection, we may feel like we're going crazy, and we indulge in a hustle or behaviours that are not typical for us. (e.g. Some hire private investigators or stalk their ex-partners. Some people message, text, or call constantly, creep on webpages, snoop in emails, and more, looking for answers).

We experience heartbreak. Many of us feel physically unwell during this time. Everything is disrupted—physically and emotionally. We don't sleep, eat, move in our lives as well as typical. The pain is pervasive and intrusive.

You will notice some changes in yourself during this stage. Your ability to concentrate, remember, and think clearly will diminish. Some report living in a 'daze,' while others report feeling exhausted and unable to participate in their lives in meaningful ways. For some, this stage leaves us unable to cry, and for others, we fear the tears will never end. This is all very normal. The shock stage is how the body distances itself from the pain. It may last for days, and it may linger in some way for months. Be gentle with yourself, you are going to be okay.

Stage 2 - *Wrestle* - In some ways, this is more of a process than a stage because it's here we struggle with our new normal. And that struggle can be a lengthy, knock-down-drag-out battle as we find our footing. The push and pull can feel oppressive and may lead to periods of hustling, negotiating, promising, and even begging.

If you are in this stage, please be especially patient with yourself. You are coming to terms with things, and navigating this new reality will take time. For me, I wrestled for many months. Some wrestle for years. Have grace with yourself as you continue to move forward through this especially difficult part of the valley.

Stage 3 - Recovery - This is the hope-filled stage as we hunker down into work-mode. It's at this time in the process that we take control back after the rejection. The first two stages leave us feeling powerless, while this stage is a getting-back-on-my-feet-ready-for-action phase. It's not pain-free, not at all. But it's liberating, and the forward momentum feels empowering and inspiring.

Not all rejections feel the same. What influences the length of recovery time?

- **Proximity.** This refers to the emotional closeness of the relationship. For example, a rejection from a colleague you don't know well feels very different than your lifelong girlfriend walking away. Emotional intimacy is on a spectrum, and the depth of emotional intimacy you share with the person influences your healing process and recovery time.

- **Investment.** This refers to how emotionally, physically, financially, and personally invested you are in the relationship. The more we have invested, the more we have to lose.

- **Trauma.** This refers to the nature of the rejection. What was said to us, about us, and what happened or is happening in the relationship before, during, and after the rejection impacts the recovery.

Looking back at my younger self, early in this recovery process still makes me cry. She wrestled hard with the rejection story. There were many days she thought she would be swallowed up by the pain. And while I can still cry for her and her pain, my tears today reflect awe and gratitude for what God did.

And if I'm honest, I'm really proud of her. In her pain and confusion, she gathered up her courage, and with broken heart in tow, she followed her Father's voice. As she did, the broken bits mended, and the pain points healed—revealing a recovery story that can only be attributed to an invested and loving God.

> God is in the business of repurposing broken things and making them beautiful again.

He does His best work in our brokenness. He heals and restores His children. And while rejection indeed leaves its mark, God is in the business of repurposing broken things and making them beautiful again. Even more beautiful than before.

KEY TAKEAWAYS

- Every recovery process is unique.

- Comparison stunts healing.

- The pivot point is the moment God reminds you that you have a choice. A choice to listen to the lies of rejection or listen to His truth.

- Rejection recovery is a process that moves us through 3 stages: Shock, Wrestle, and Recovery.

- God is in the business of repurposing broken things and making them beautiful.   Revelation 21:5

REJECTION RECOVERY

But now, this is what the Lord says—he who created you, Jacob, he who formed you, Israel: 'Do not fear, for I have redeemed you; I have summoned you by name; you are mine. When you pass through the waters, I will be with you; and when you pass through the rivers, they will not sweep over you. When you walk through the fire, you will not be burned; the flames will not set you ablaze (Isaiah 43:1-2).

THERAPEUTIC QUESTIONS

- What stage of this process do you find yourself in?
- What obstacles may keep you from moving forward?
- Your pivot point requires a choice. What choice do you make today to begin your journey away from rejection and toward recovery?
- If you could have coffee with Jesus, what suggestions would He have for you as you take your first steps toward His new life for you?

JOURNAL PROMPT

What does rejection resiliency mean to you? What truths does God have to say about you?

Heavenly Father, I know recovery starts with a choice. I choose You. I choose to turn away from my pain story and focus on You. Help me Jesus. I need Your reminders that I am not in this alone. I trust You to be with me through this valley. You say in Your Word that You are with me. Please help me to seek You and focus on You and Your promises. I want to recover from this rejection. I know You declare me unrejectable and fully acceptable. Thank You for loving me and for the healing work You are starting in my life. I love you, Lord. Amen.

CHAPTER 3

The Co-Accusers

"Not everything that is faced can be changed, but nothing can be changed until it is faced."

—JAMES BALDWIN

Three months into the valley—ninety-two days after my husband said he was done—I wrote the following words: *I am totally, irreparably broken. It hurts to breathe, and all I can think about is "why?". Why has this happened? What is wrong with me? Am I really that unlovable? And who am I now? Jesus, please help me. I wear a scarlet letter everyone can see. How can I do life now?*

Do you see the sinister message woven in this journal entry? One person chose to walk away—and with that singular action—the door opened to a litany of evil heavy-hitters. When rejection came on the scene, it brought shame and anxiety. It introduced grief like I'd never known before. And it shoved self-esteem, identity, and hope to the floor. Rejection does not act alone. If it did, it wouldn't hurt as much.

Rejection is painful. But what I discovered in my research is the majority of pain caused by rejection comes from co-accusers and the messages of torment that get spun as a result. Let me explain.

> Rejection is an action against us, and in and of itself, it means nothing.

Rejection is an action against us, and in and of itself, it means nothing. Rejection is powerless until we attach meaning to it.

It's the onslaught of emotions, and beliefs accompanying the rejection that hold the most pain for us. I call these the co-accusers: additional messages, emotions, and beliefs that rush in on the heels of a rejection. They always add insult to injury. And in every case, seek to fill our hearts with lies.

When rejection came calling on me a few years ago, it brought with it a team of co-accusers. Anxiety, shame, and grief packed the greatest punch, filling my mind with toxic messages. And I became obsessed with rehearsing my pain story. It made me feel small, and it threatened to completely drain me of my self-esteem. Maybe you know exactly what I'm talking about here.

Co-accusers lie to us. They lie about our worth, our strengths, our abilities and our future. I wrestled hard with them, and I'm going to guess you have too. Maybe you're still wrestling. Rejection is not the enemy. The enemy is the harmful stories and lies that spin in our minds as we interpret the rejection. These stories and lies are the tactics of the co-accusers who hold the sole objective of keeping us stuck in the valley.

I have found there are common co-accusers recruited by rejection. The list below is not exhaustive, and you may face additional and equally troublesome teammates. Please be gentle with yourself as you navigate through this list, remember to hold tight to the truth, and be reminded how deeply you are loved. *"And may you have the power to understand, as all God's people should, how wide, how long, how high, and how deep his love is"* (Ephesians 3:18 NLT).

Shame

This is the right-hand best friend of Rejection. It's a persistent, corrosive, and private pain. Of all the difficult emotions we face, shame has the ability to knock us to our knees and keep us there. As you navigate this valley, keep a keen eye out for this sinister enemy of healing.

Many people have written about shame over the years, and my personal favorite, Brene Brown, says, *"I define shame as the intensely painful feeling or experience of believing that we are flawed and therefore unworthy of love and belonging—something we've experienced, done, or failed to do makes us unworthy of connection. I don't believe shame is helpful or productive. In fact, I think shame is much more likely to be the source of destructive, hurtful behavior than the solution or cure."*[1]

Shame declares us unworthy of love. It holds us hostage in a story of inadequacy and seeks to isolate us, convincing us that our isolation is a way to emotionally protect others. *What will people think if they find out who I really am? My past makes me unlovable and unacceptable.*

Are you battling the co-accuser Shame? Have a look at the list below. Do you see yourself in any of these statements? If so, shame is a co-accuser you will want to address.

- ☐ I wish I could just disappear.
- ☐ I feel powerless or worthless.
- ☐ I recite self-blaming and self-loathing words to myself about myself.
- ☐ I feel angry a lot and am defensive and reactive when criticized.
- ☐ I rarely ask for help.
- ☐ I am quite critical of others.
- ☐ I can't let myself get close to people or trust them.
- ☐ I believe I deserve the bad things that have happened to me.

Anxiety

This oh-so-common co-accuser has us reciting what-ifs, should'ves, and regret-laden mental narratives. It awfulizes the future and feeds us the bad news story at every turn. Anxiety keeps us up at night, wakes us when we sleep and travels with us through every aspect of the day.

Are you battling the co-accuser Anxiety? Review the list below and check all that apply.

- ☐ I am constantly worrying about things.
- ☐ I'm easily annoyed or overwhelmed.
- ☐ I'm so restless it's hard to sit still.
- ☐ I have physical symptoms, such as racing heart, trouble breathing, upset stomach, or ringing ears.
- ☐ I feel irrational and overreact to situations and people.
- ☐ I have trouble falling asleep and staying asleep.
- ☐ I can't concentrate on anything.
- ☐ I feel on edge and emotional.

Grief

When we are rejected by someone we love, the grief is compounded by the story of choice. The story *they chose to walk away* leaves us to not only grieve their absence in our lives, we are also left to grieve what we thought was true of ourselves—that we are wanted, loved and chosen.

Grief is one of the most complex human experiences and addressing it is absolutely part of rejection recovery. Sadly, rejection does not afford us the opportunity for a pure grieving process, and that's why it makes it on the list of co-accusers.

Grief from rejection blames and accuses, insisting we don't deserve to grieve. This silences us. And because those around us don't know how to interact with our grief, it compounds the isolation and shame we feel.

Are you battling the co-accuser Grief? Have a look at the list and check all that apply to you.

- ☐ I think so much about the person who left that I can't think of much else.
- ☐ I feel I can't accept the loss of the person who left.
- ☐ I feel disbelief that they left.
- ☐ I feel distant from and disinterested in others.
- ☐ I don't care about things the way I used to.
- ☐ I feel envious of others who have not lost someone they love.
- ☐ I am on an emotional rollercoaster—sometimes sad, sometimes angry.
- ☐ I avoid anything that might trigger a memory of that person.

Anger

The U.S. Surgeon General issued a report stating that in 2011, rejection was a greater risk for adolescent violence than drugs, poverty, or gang membership. Recent research suggests that rejection and the fear of rejection is the reason for considerable maladaptive behaviours in youth and adults.[2]

Even mild rejections lead people to take out their aggression on innocent bystanders. School shootings, violence against women, and fired workers going "postal" are other examples of the strong link between rejection and aggression.

Anger is one of the most demanding emotions. And in many cases, it seeks a physical outlet. But if you're like me, anger sits percolating on the inside, building a fortress of negativity, and holding us hostage to self-deprecating, hostile messages.

Are you battling this co-accuser anger? Have a look at the list below, and check all that apply.

- ☐ I feel irritable and on edge all the time.
- ☐ I can't organize my thoughts or my life like I used to.
- ☐ I snap and lash out.
- ☐ I experience headaches and body aches from being tense.
- ☐ Sometimes I think about hurting myself or the person who hurt me.
- ☐ I have noticed my words are sharp and I've become abrupt.
- ☐ I feel less tolerant of others, and sometimes don't even like them.
- ☐ I have rage fantasies often where I unload my emotion on someone.

Resentment, Bitterness, and Pride

Resentment, bitterness, and pride are the score-keepers. They collect wrongs, focus on shortcomings, and seek division. On the surface, these poisonous co-accusers might make us feel powerful, but ultimately keep us stuck in the pain.

When left unmanaged, this pain triangle leaves us edgy, sharp, and angry people. Poisonous and stealthy, resentment enters the soul after an injustice, betrayal, misunderstanding, or rejection. Left to itself, the insidious effects of resentment slowly eat away at our lives, leaving hatred to boil over and leak angry outbursts with a harmful outpouring of poison. Resentment is the most dangerous and harmful of all the co-accusers, and it can sometimes show up as anger, indifference, or contempt. It's tricky because while this may on some level feel powerful and leave us feeling *in control*, resentment actually has us giving up control to others. Namely, the person who has hurt us.

Are you battling the co-accusers Resentment, Bitterness and Pride? Review the list below and check those that apply.

- ☐ I am focused on the injustice and the wrong done to me.
- ☐ I generalize. (e.g. *all men are cheaters, I can't trust anyone.*)
- ☐ I hold grudges and don't let things go.
- ☐ I talk a lot about the injustice and the wrongness of what's happened, and I talk a lot about myself.
- ☐ I struggle to accept advice, feedback, teaching and correction.
- ☐ I don't affirm, encourage, or celebrate others easily.
- ☐ I don't ask for help.
- ☐ Cheerful, easy-going people bother me.
- ☐ I use sarcasm a lot.

Depression

Creeping in slowly on the heels of anxiety, isolation, and resentment, this co-accuser seeks to completely shut us down. Sadness, if left unattended, can build into depression, creating a lens that darkens all aspects of our lives and keeps us from engaging in a life we enjoy—a life God has for us.

This very serious co-accuser stands in opposition to God's Truth. And for many people, requires clinical care to address. If I can highlight anything in this section, it's this fact—there is no shame in needing clinical or medical support to address depression. During my particularly difficult time in the valley, I felt my sadness becoming deeper and darker. There were days it felt like it might swallow me whole, and I wondered if I would ever feel okay again. If you are feeling this way, please have a chat with your family doctor and a qualified Christian counselor. You may need to explore the option of medication during this part of the journey and my friend, that is absolutely okay.

If you check more than three of the following and have been feeling this way for longer than three months, please consult a professional counselor.

Are you battling the co-accuser Depression?

- ☐ I feel hopeless and helpless.
- ☐ I have lost my appetite or am hungry all the time.
- ☐ I can't sleep, or I need to sleep all the time.
- ☐ I have unexplained aches and pains.
- ☐ I am highly emotional—I cry a lot, am irritable and angry.
- ☐ I lack emotion and feel flat and disinterested.
- ☐ I can't concentrate.
- ☐ I have no energy and feel physically heavy.
- ☐ I hate myself and speak to myself harshly.

Comparison

This grossly unfair co-accuser has us measuring our lives and our stories up against others. Comparison has us judging in favor of others and keeps us focused on what we've lost. It feeds jealousy, competition, rivalry, and in many cases turns friends into enemies, because we resent what they have. Comparison breeds the illusion of perfectionism, and it has us measuring up against what we believe is perfect in others.

Are you battling the co-accuser Comparison? Consider the following indicators, and check all that apply.

- ☐ I struggle to think positively of myself.
- ☐ I am jealous of the opportunities of others.
- ☐ I can't see how God could use me anymore.
- ☐ I am constantly doubting myself and my worth.
- ☐ I measure myself up against others and their experiences.
- ☐ I notice others' strengths and abilities, and then I criticize myself.
- ☐ I focus on my shortcomings, berate myself, and glorify others.
- ☐ I spend a lot of time on social media looking into other people's lives.

From Victim to Victor

While rejection is painful, it is not the source of our greatest pain. The agony brought about by the messages and lies of each of the co-accusers is especially debilitating, and it is a call to action. Knowing the enemy we are fighting makes our tactics more effective. Consider the following strategies to address the lies that may be spinning in your heart, and use them to establish a victory stance in the face of the enemy.

1. Name your co-accuser. If it's shame, call it out.
   "*I recognize you shame. I see what you're trying to do.*"

2. Tell it *no*. This is a clinical strategy to stop unwelcome thoughts from impacting our feelings. Say, "*You are not welcome here. I refuse to engage in shame-based thinking.*"

3. Remind the co-accuser of the truth. Just because rejection has happened, does not make you unwanted or unlovable. It does not need to lead you into comparison, shame-based thinking, anger, or more. "*I am deeply loved by the King of the Universe. I was created on purpose, for a purpose. God has amazing things in store for me. I am chosen.*"

4. Recite scripture, read the Bible out loud, and play worship music. I suggest developing a playlist of your favorite worship songs and listening to it regularly.

As Christians, we know the messages brought about by rejection are not from God. They are in direct conflict with what He says about us. So, confronting these lies with truth is essential to reducing the long-term impact of rejection. When left unaddressed, the co-accusers interrupt the healing journey God has designed for us and take us off course and away from the truth. As we navigate this valley together, let's commit to keep our hearts fully locked on the words of our Heavenly Father and the truth He declares about us—we are highly favoured, chosen and adored. No human can take that away from us. Ever.

KEY TAKEAWAYS

- Rejection does not act alone nor is it the most painful part of this experience.

- The shame-based messages we internalize and recite create the most pain.

- Co-accusers are the painful teammates of rejection who feed the lies and messages determined to bring further harm, keeping us from healing and knowing God's will for our lives.

- God has a unique plan for each of us. This valley experience is where we can draw closer to Him, and where He will reveal important truths about Who He is, and who we are to Him.

- The co-accusers do not hold truth about us.

John 8 44-47

REJECTION RECOVERY

> *See what great love the Father has lavished on us, that we should be called the children of God! And that is what we are!* (1 John 3:1a).

THERAPEUTIC QUESTIONS

- When rejection came calling, what co-accusers did it recruit for the team?

- If these co-accusers were benched, kicked off the team, or no longer able to taunt you, how would your life be different?

- What rules does this problem have you following? And what rules might you consider breaking? For me, the rule was to focus on my loss and ruminate on the hurtful things said to me. When I broke this rule and stopped focusing on the loss and the mean words, I shifted my focus onto the truth and the future.

- Is it fair that rejection thinks it can bully you with this group of co-accusers?? Why or why not?

JOURNAL PROMPT

Who does God say I am? List ten things He says that are in conflict with what the co-accusers have me believing.

Heavenly Father, please protect me from these co-accusers. Help me to notice them, challenge them with Your truth, and trust You with the healing. I don't want to be sensitive to the impact of rejection and the things it tells me. I want to be sensitive to You, and what You say about me. Thank you that Your Words of me are truth I can trust. Amen.

CHAPTER 4

War Wounds and Battle Scars

"If we are to nurture and heal, we must admit that the wounds exist."

—IYANLA VANZANT

I left a really mean note on her windshield. In fact, it was more than mean. I'm embarrassed to tell you what it said—it was rude. At twenty-two, I was debilitated by a cocktail of shame, anger, and grief dragging me through life.

On this particular day, an elderly woman made the fateful decision to take up two parking spots near the mall entrance. Unfortunately for her (oh, how I cringe as I write this), my angry younger self needed a place to unleash the brokenness and pain. My nasty note heaped the shame I felt onto her, berating this unsuspecting, innocent woman, and probably leaving her feeling verbally abused for the day. Or maybe longer.

How do I know that this car belonged to an elderly woman? Because after tucking the note indignantly under the windshield wiper, I started my march toward the mall entrance where she was standing out of the rain, watching me. She smiled a beautiful smile, and bags in hand, made her way toward her car. Toward my note. A note from an angry young woman with a chip on her shoulder, who was about to ruin her day.

As I write this, I am embarrassed about my behaviour. It was completely out of character for me. Correction, through a number of jagged-edged years, it had become my character. Dabbling in toxic choices as a teenager a few years prior to this m*ean note* incident, had resulted in mass rejection by my closest Christian friends. As if on cue, when my friends walked out one door, shame entered through another. It brought a myriad of co-accusers, threatening to steal away who I knew myself to be, and infused the remaining bits with bitterness.

By the time I was twenty-two, I didn't recognize myself anymore. And in my pain, I made a big, life-changing decision—I ran away from home. It didn't take much to convince myself that running away was a gift to my family and friends—a way to protect them from the choices I was making. But in all honesty, this runaway was completely shame-laden. Looking into the eyes of my parents, my peers, and my own reflection became unbearable.

Today, almost thirty years later, I can still feel my heart ache, as that broken young woman hugged her parents goodbye, pointed her car west, and drove away.

Shame grew into a blistering infection that controlled everything I did, collecting story after story to prove its point. Like a dark passenger, shame's oppressive voice spewed a loathsome narrative into my heart that declared me dirty, unlovable, rejectable, and bad to my core.

This is the cruel mission of rejection, isn't it? Ultimately, rejection, if we embrace it, gets inflamed, brings its co-accusers into the mix, depletes us of our self-esteem and hope, and then leads us toward more trouble. When we don't feel good about ourselves, but instead believe that we are not deserving of good things, or can't trust anyone, we start to see ourselves as *less-than*, alone, replaceable.

The Cycle of Rejection

The Cycle of Rejection

- Rejected
- Increased shame, grief + anger / Decreased self-esteem, trust + hope
- Harmful Choices/Behaviours
- More shame, grief, anger, and now added resentment

Battle Scars

Rejection and its co-accusers leave a mark. I tried to convince myself that the marks were invisible, that I could hide them. But looking back, I see my younger self, the twenty-two-year-old me, leaving notes of bitterness for innocent people, or the forty-five-year-old me, distancing myself from friends who enjoyed a married life I no longer had. I see that while I thought I had addressed the co-accusers, the evidence said otherwise.

Some battle scars were hidden, but they still informed my behaviours. Did I have revenge fantasies? Yes, indeed. Did the rejection story wake me up in the middle of the night with self-loathing chatter and cynicism about God's goodness? Yes. Rejection recovery is a process. And part of the process is noticing the wounds, healing them, and moving forward. Time and time again.

While this is not an exhaustive list of battle scars, what I'm going to share does reflect the most common ones women bring to counseling. I'll discuss each briefly here. But if you find yourself bearing any of these scars, I encourage you to consider connecting with a caring, Christian therapist who can walk you through the steps to healing.

Battle Scar #1 - *Lowered Self-esteem*

The first, and perhaps most painful, wound—rejection—is a blow to our self-esteem. When we experience rejection, we immediately grapple with our worth. Low self-esteem leaves us believing we are unlovable, incompetent, and undeserving of good things. And in many cases, it leads to hypersensitivity—leaving us with a fragile sense of self and more vulnerable to additional wounding. This hypersensitivity puts us on high alert to further signs of rejection, causing us to anticipate or interpret unacceptance, even when there is none.

Fear of further rejection or perceived failure puts us on guard, observing our own behaviours through a critical lens. We behave more defensively, and even lash out. Of considerable concern is the ongoing internal narrative that continues to criticize and berate us when we make a mistake. While the experience of rejection is hard on self-esteem, our critical inner voice and the nasty narrative in our heads has the most painful impact. The words we say to ourselves—about ourselves—matter.

Battle Scar #2 - *Dependence/Neediness*

Rejection can breed a sense of desperation for acceptance, driving us to lean heavily on our relationships to fill the gaps left behind by rejection. Looking to others for validation of our worth leads to disappointment and perpetuates this cycle.

Battle Scar #3 - *Co-Dependence*

This is a complex behavioural condition within a relationship, where one person organizes their entire life around pleasing the other person, losing their own identity in the process. When our self-esteem and sense of self is reliant totally on acceptance by the other person, we are left to feel worthless if he or she rejects us. This problem can exist in any of our relationships. And when we have experienced rejection, we may find ourselves more susceptible to co-dependent behaviours and relationships in the future.

Battle Scar #4 - *Extreme Independence*

This is a sneaky wound left behind by ongoing experiences with rejection. Some experts suggest that it's a trauma response, creating an inability to trust anyone, including ourselves. And the results in an *us versus them* approach to life. When people let us down by not following through with promises, walking away, or turning their backs on us, we learn that we can't rely on anyone else. We fear more hurt, more disappointment, and heartbreak. So, we refuse help, go it alone, and shut people out. The guardedness that results, though rooted in self-preservation, actually turns against us and leaves us lonelier and more isolated than the rejection itself.

Battle Scar #5 - *Imperfectionism and Perfectionism*

The message we hear from rejection is that we are unacceptable and deeply flawed. And for many of us, that message drives us toward a life focused on living perfectly. While for others, it has us throwing in the towel and engaging in self-destructive life choices.

What you may not know is that following the path of least resistance is often the path of most pain. The destructive behaviour that follows a significant rejection is rooted in the belief that we are not worthy of good things. On the other hand, perfectionism is a function of anxiety and drives us to pursue the impossible. Many wrestle hard with perfectionism, which holds them hostage in a self-deprecating cycle of *shoulds*, all or nothing thinking, and an unflinching focus on flaws. Striving for perfection in hopes of avoiding further rejection does not help us heal. Burnout is inevitable for perfectionists, followed by depression.

Battle Scar # 6 – *Guardedness and Rigid Boundaries*

Rooted in the fear of additional rejection, guardedness and rigid boundaries have us make promises to ourselves, like, *I will never trust again. I will never let anyone get close to me. I will never love anyone or be vulnerable with anyone again.* While this may certainly protect us from further rejection, it also limits connection and the possibility of the joy that comes from being close to someone.

Battle Scar #7 - *Fear and Cynicism*

This combination makes for a lonely and isolated life, and they are enemies to change. These war wounds promote a distaste for connection and can create unfair, untrue stories to reduce possible exposure to pain.

Fear-based thinking is problem-focused and keeps its sights set on the *what-ifs*. *What if that happens again? What if that person is going to leave me too? What if he's lying to me?* Cynicism, on the other hand, predicts awfulized outcomes and anticipates the worst in people. We convince ourselves that this protects us from further rejection when in reality it only sets us up for isolation, disconnection, and more pain.

Battle Scar #8 - *Depression*

I often say that depression is the big brother of sad. We all feel sad from time to time; and rejection definitely brings tremendous sadness. But left unattended, sad morphs into depression. At the root of many stories of depression, is the feeling of not being accepted, wanted, or loved.

Depression feels unbearably heavy and draws us away from things that have brought us joy in the past. This is a very serious mental health concern. If you find yourself feeling depressed, please connect with a mental health professional right away.

Battle Scar #9 - *Self-doubt and Comparison*

These two often show up together. Self-doubt is a mental habit that gains momentum when we experience rejection. Losing a relationship inevitably causes us to question our choices, our value, or our behaviours. Losing something of significance leaves us wondering about our ability to perform well and keep things we value. The personal narrative spinning in our heads about our ability to make good decisions and behave properly perpetuates the problem of trusting ourselves.

Comparison is the thief of joy. Rejection, especially by a spouse, catapults us into an acute noticing of what other people have. And then props it up beside what we no longer have and rubs our nose in it. We become judge and jury, resenting people for having what they have and assessing whether or not they're deserving of it.

Comparison breeds bitterness and embraces an us-versus-them mentality, separating us from further connection and embedding the scars of rejection deeper into our hearts.

Battle Scar #10 - *Self-rejection*

This is an extreme battle scar and a common problem resulting from rejection. When we buy into the message that we are indeed rejectable and believe the things said to us and about us, we villainize ourselves based on the behaviour and opinions of others. This is what I refer to as a thickening problem. It starts as a noticing, and then thickens into a bigger, more troublesome issue.

Self-rejection prompts destructive behaviours and creates sharp, jagged edges in us, causing us to harm ourselves and others.

Battle Scar #11 - *Resentment and Bitterness*

This poisonous team settles in after we've spent some time in the valley. They collect and stockpile real and imagined wrongs against us and inform our attitudes and interactions with others. Every single time, this team of pain-makers separates us from others, isolates us, and brings despair. If left to their own devices, resentment and bitterness make us difficult people to be around.

Battle Scar #12 - *Anxiety*

This often shows up either as fear of abandonment, creating over attachments and neediness, or as fear of connection, creating guardedness and convincing us that trusting others is unsafe.

Anxiety, if unaddressed, can wreak havoc in our lives. Demanding and fear-focused, it exaggerates and awfulizes the future, convincing us to believe we are ill-equipped and unprepared. Anxiety always tells us the bad news story and keeps us focused on what-ifs and should-haves.

Now the Good News

Rejection invites us into a unique experience with pain. We get to choose whether or not we will accept the invitation. If we fully indulge it, rejection can drive us through an emotional spin cycle of self-deprecation, resulting in a deeper experience with pain.

Never neat and tidy, rejection by its very nature brings turmoil. Devastating things are said that can't be unsaid. Awful, life-changing choices are made for us, leaving a ripple effect in our lives. The painful truth is that someone you love has walked away, leaving you with battle scars you did not ask for.

> The war wounds and battle scars are part of your story, but they are not the most important parts.

Here's the good news—we get to choose how deep these scars go. The war wounds and battle scars are part of your story, but they are not the most important parts. When we stare too long at our injuries, we pick up the torch of rejection and keep the flame burning. We must not carry the torch.

Every day we recite the nasty narrative, we pick up that torch and obey the rules of rejection, forfeiting our freedom. When there's been an injustice or a painful undoing of our lives, wounds and scars are part of the deal. We all bear them. But healing is possible.

God has called us to be free. Free from the oppressive nature of these scars. Free from reciting the nasty narratives that hold us hostage. These scars and wounds are in direct conflict with His plans for us. Dropping the rejection torch and releasing the wounded ways of walking through the valley, we find Him ready with healing words of love and reminders of His thoughts about us. Freedom from this pain is possible. On the other side of the valley, I believe you will look back and see what you have travelled through—what God has brought you out of. He is the Great Physician, fully capable of healing your heart, mind, and soul.

KEY TAKEAWAYS

- Rejection leaves battle scars and war wounds that can isolate us and keep us disconnected from others.

- The scars and wounds get infected, taking root and festering, if we don't address them and give them over to God.

- We can choose to carry the torch given to us by rejection, or lay it down and pursue the healing hands of Jesus.

- God is the Great Physician, ready and able to heal our wounds.

Pslam 118:22

Luke 10:16

REJECTION RECOVERY

Do not be anxious about anything, but in everything by prayer and petition, with thanksgiving, present your requests to God. And the peace of God, which transcends all understanding will guard your hearts and your minds in Christ Jesus (Philippians 4:6-7).

THERAPEUTIC QUESTIONS

- What war wounds and battle scars are the most painful in your story?
- Given what you know about God, what would He say about these battle scars?
- The rejection story wants you to carry the torch and keep the flame burning. Why does it want that for you?
- What would happen if you put the torch down and broke the rules of these war wounds?

JOURNAL PROMPT

What do you think God wants you to know about how He feels about you?

Jesus, I need Your healing. The leftovers from this rejection have me spinning. I want to believe what You say about me. I need You to reach through this pain, and remind me of Your healing, Your words and Your truths. I am blessed and highly favoured. Help me to walk in that Truth, and stop reciting the pain story. Thank you for comforting me, and staying with me in this dark valley. I will follow You. Amen.

CHAPTER 5

Rejection is a Liar

"I'm always disappointed when a liar's pants don't actually catch on fire."

—U<small>NKNOWN</small>

Sporting a high-end Lulu outfit under her stylish jean jacket she almost bounced into the waiting area. Her dark brown hair held loose curls resting perfectly on her shoulders, and her smile showed the room a set of brilliantly white, perfectly straight teeth. Claire lit up the room when she arrived—this eighteen-year-old woman seemed to have it all together.

I felt an instant connection as we introduced ourselves prior to her counseling session. When she turned that beautiful smile toward me, I was caught off guard. Behind a full set of dark lashes sat the saddest blue eyes I had ever seen.

While her smile tried to tell me everything was okay, her eyes gave away the pain in her heart. There was almost nothing in her gaze. I searched for feeling in her face, but her eyes were completely flat, almost hollow. She followed me confidently down the hall and through my office door. I motioned for her to have a seat, and as she did, she grabbed the Kleenex® box on the coffee table, curled up on the couch, and wept. Despair was enormous in the room, and as Claire let herself come unglued, the space between us filled with emotion she had held onto for years.

There were moments Claire lifted her head to speak, mascara mixed with tears of brokenness covering her face. Her breathing was laboured, as she tried to collect herself. But the tears still came, so she just let them. She gave in to the grief. And as we sat together, my heart knew her pain.

I understood this girl more than she knew. And my guess is, you do too. Without even knowing the origin of her pain and the reason for her heartache, we can connect with it. That's the thing about heartbreak and devastation, isn't it? We all get it. We've had knees to chest moments where the tears flush out some of the pain, and without words, our hearts just empty through our eyes.

Claire had a broken heart. Her father had walked away from the family when she was two years old, and she had not seen him since that day. Although her memories of him are few, she thinks about him every day. And she always has. Financial hardships meant Claire and her Mom lived in shelters and apartments that were not safe for either of them. When Claire was four years old, her mother married a wealthy man who was much older, but who offered a comfortable life with a promise of a safe place to live. Claire did not find safety in this home though. For several years, this man who shared a bed with her mother sexually abused Claire, sometimes on a daily basis.

When Claire was fourteen, she met her boyfriend and moved in with his family, a caring, Christian family who welcomed her as their own. Because of their kindness, Claire had a safe space to work through some of the historical pain she was carrying. Eventually, Claire found the incredible courage to face the man who had abused her for many years. She courageously saw him brought to justice.

Claire's arrival in my office was six months after she testified in court. Her Mother was enraged by her decision and disowned Claire on that day. Parentless, wounded, and scared, Claire clung to her knees in my office, certain she would never feel loved again. The shame and fear she carried declared her unworthy of belonging. In the safety of the counseling space, Claire shared her plans to take her own life.

This beautiful young woman carried a facade of confidence but held a plan in her heart to end her life that day. Counseling was her last-ditch attempt to find hope. Tormented by a rejection story spanning sixteen years, Claire decided she was unworthy of love and undeserving of happiness.

If you had met Claire that day, you would have stood with me in protest against the rejection story that tried to kill her. You would have shaken your head in disbelief that this beautiful woman who held such potential could possibly believe this rejection story. If you sat with us that day, you would have heard Claire say she was a burden, unlovable, and not enough. You would have held space for her, as I did, and heard the rejection story ooze lies about her worth and value. And you would have put your arm around her, insisting this cruel narrative about her was not true.

Because it's not true of Claire. And it's not true of you, either.

The Lies We Can't Believe and the Rules We Must Break

The lies Claire believed are the same lies you and I have believed. These lies of our rejectability, our worthlessness, and our hopelessness are in direct conflict with what God says about us. The lies seek to draw us away from the life-giving Truth from our Heavenly Father.

You may relate to the following list of lies and rules that tormented me during the first several months of my recovery. Take a few moments to consider the ones oppressing you today.

Lie #1 - I am deeply flawed and inadequate.

Rule #1 - Be small and remain hidden and passive, or inflate and be aggressive.

Lie #2 - I am undeserving of _____ (love, loyalty, healthy relationship, commitment, and more).

Rule #2 - Avoid connection, don't trust, be cynical, and focus on my shortcomings. Notice others' behaviours toward me and assess their disinterest to prove the lie.

Lie #3 - I will never get over this. It will always hurt.

Rule #3 - Focus on the loss, ignore the blessings, and remember all of the pain.

Lie #4 - God doesn't want me.

Rule #4 - Don't open the Bible—withdraw from time with God.

Lie #5 - Other people think I am a failure. If they knew, they would reject me too.

Rule #4 - Withdraw, reduce contact and vulnerability. Don't be honest.

Out of the Dark and Into the Light

> Let's switch our focus from what is hurting us to Who is holding us.

Let's switch our focus from what is hurting us to Who is holding us. Being focused on Jesus will never do anything but better equip us for what's to come. Deficit-based thinking, or in other words, focusing on what we lack, what we've lost, or what we miss, will fill us with despair. Despair can lead to desperation, which causes us to obsess about the person who's hurt us or the situation that brings sadness.

God has made us many promises, and He is absolutely going to keep them. You've been betrayed. Someone you love betrayed you, walked away from you, or both. You have lost trust. And you're wondering if you will ever trust again. I'm over here nodding. I get that feeling. I understand this pain and the fear.

In my obsession with rejection, I declared some very pointed things to God. My journey in the valley taught me that He wants to hear from me, and He wants me to share my heart with Him. Sure, He already knows what's going on. But as a *loving* father, He wants us to tell Him. Talk to Him.

Vulnerable and broken, I got down on my knees, and I told Him everything. I gave Him all the grief and shame. I told Him how unworthy and unlovable I felt. And I told Him how angry I was—angry at everything, even Him. I remember looking up at the ceiling in my little apartment, and crying out to Him, "I don't know how I will ever trust a man again, Lord."

No lightning bolt struck me down when I got real with God. And instead of guilt, I felt reassurance. That's what He wants—our honesty and our emotion. In that moment, in His perfectly gentle way, the Holy Spirit whispered into my heart, *You don't need to worry about that right now; you just need to trust Me.*

Trust. I was running way too hard. I just needed to trust the Man Who died for me. *I can do that,* I said in my heart. I can do that. And so can you. There is no one more trustworthy. No deeper love. No safer place than in the arms of Jesus. You can trust the Man Who died for you.

The relationship we build with God will carry us through this valley. He can be trusted one hundred percent of the time. When we rest fully on Him, we can walk away from the fear and anxiety that show up with our rejection story. And when we trust what He says about us, we can wholeheartedly accept that our worth and value are not connected to our marital status or who wants us. Clinging to the truths He tells us over and over in His word—we are loved, accepted and unconditionally celebrated—we can leave behind the oppression of rejection and breath in the freedom of His truth.

In His embrace, rejection is powerless.

A Box of Lies

Here's a fun game I play when the rejection story is strong, and the lies are bearing down on me. Imagine you could box up rejection, its lies, and all of its co-accusers. Now, picture standing in front of Jesus, box in hand. In your mind, open that box up and hold it out to Him.

What do you imagine is happening in that box when it's opened up and staring into the face of the King is the Universe, the Creator of everything?

I imagine that inside that box is a writhing, screeching pile of scared and desperate things wanting to run. It brings a smile to my face to think about it.

You are the daughter of the King of Kings. Rejection wants you to forget this truth. You are loved by the Creator of the universe. Your worth and your value are not connected to anything human. You belong. One day you will stand in front of Jesus and He will call you by name, smiling from ear to ear, arms wide open, welcoming you home. Set your sights on that. It got me through many days in the valley. You belong to Jesus Christ, He chose you, He wants you just as you are and He walks with you in the valley.

KEY TAKEAWAYS

- Rejection feeds us lies and seeks to draw us away from God's truth. 🖤

- Being real with God, vulnerable, and honest is exactly what He wants.

- God is not surprised by your struggle and not offended by your wrestle.

- You are chosen by Jesus. He wants you, and He is willing to travel this journey with you.

- You have a new name: Daughter of the King.

Peter 2:9-19
Deuteromy 7:6-8

REJECTION RECOVERY

Even though the fig trees have no blossoms, and there are no grapes on the vines; even though the olive crop fails, and the fields lie empty and barren; even though the flocks die in the fields, and the cattle barns are empty, yet I will rejoice in the Lord! I will be joyful in the God of my salvation! The Sovereign Lord is my strength! He makes me as surefooted as a deer, able to tread upon the heights (Habakkuk 3:17-19 NLT).

THERAPEUTIC QUESTIONS

- What lies does rejection have you believing about yourself?

- If you were to pack those lies up in a box, and show them to Jesus, what would He say about them?

- In what ways does your title Daughter of the King of Kings help you stand against the lies of rejection?

- If rejection and Jesus had a conversation about you, how would that go?

JOURNAL PROMPT

What lies does rejection want you to believe about yourself? What does God say about you? Write out the truth.

Thank you, Lord, for reminding me of the Truth. The alluring story of rejection has had me believing harmful stories that are not true of me. I am choosing to believe what You say, Jesus. Your truth covers any lies from rejection. Give me the wisdom to intercept these lies when they show up, and help me to keep my eyes focused fully on You when things get blurry. Thank you for loving me and travelling with me through this valley. Amen.

PART 2

The R Words that Heal

CHAPTER 6

Relished

"What a mercy it is that it is not your hold of Christ that saves you, but His hold of you."

—C.H. Spurgeon

I woke with a tightness in my chest that had become a familiar, but unwanted travel companion. *Rejected. Rejected. Rejectable.* Weary and heartsore, I got out of bed to start my day. The words continued to run through my mind like a Tasmanian devil, *Rejected. Rejectable. Unwanted.* This battle exhausted me.

I clenched my teeth, and begged, *Jesus, please help me*! I felt a tear slip off my chin and watched as it disappeared into the plush area rug at my feet. Was I this forgettable? Could I so easily be let go to disappear and be forgotten? Anxiety rose in my chest and I struggled to breathe. *Jesus, please, I need help!*

I don't know about you, but sometimes I am stopped in my tracks by a thought or a pull in my heart that can only come from Jesus. Sometimes it starts with noticing something I am certain God is drawing my attention to, or an awareness of His nudge. On this particular day, I had a sense in my soul that felt like He was right there with me.

I imagined Him as He spoke. With a gentle, knowing smile on His face, I heard God whisper in my heart, *You sure love R words, Nicole. Why don't you go write down all the R words you can think of?*

I need you to understand that I really had never heard God clearly before this day. I believed He did in fact speak to people, but I doubted He would talk to me directly. Prior to this moment, He had shown me His nearness and investment more subtly. He drew my attention to certain Scripture, opened closed doors in my life, and even provided peace when the anxiety was raging. But this day was different.

One of my favorite things about Jesus is that He knows His kids so well. He speaks exactly as we need Him to in ways we can understand. I love words. God knows better than anyone that using words to connect with me is most effective. His divine interruption, when He spoke to me that day, was about to change everything.

I settled into my favorite blue-plush chair, where I did my devotions every morning. Opening my journal, I started to write every R word that came to my mind. One of the first ones?

Yes, you betcha—Rejection. I wrote it big and bold, and I circled it several times, as if trying to make a point. I felt prompted to keep writing.

Okay God. Redneck, Rubbish, REJECTED, Rude, Rhubarb. Come on, God, what's this about?

Relish. This word stopped me right there, pen in hand.

Somehow, I knew He was not referring to the favored condiment you might put on your hot dog or in potato salad. God's voice was gentle in my soul. *Look it up.*

When I opened the dictionary, I could not believe what I read. Among other things, according to Merriam-Webster Dictionary, relished is defined as: *a pleasing or zestful flavor, to delight in something, vigorous and enthusiastic enjoyment, loved, and adored.*[3]

Weeping with overflowing joy, I leapt out of my chair. I sang and danced in circles around my living room. *Adored!* What a beautiful word. In my wrestling and my new found obsession with rejection, I had completely lost sight of my adorable-ness. As is common with rejection, it collects and stockpiles other examples of rejection in our lives, and it has us rehashing memories of times we felt uninvited, not chosen, and unwanted. These messages clog up the truth filters, leaving us focused on our reject-ability, rather than on our adorability. But Jesus adores us. He finds us adorable.

In that pivotal living room moment with Jesus, everything changed. My husband had still walked away, claiming he no longer loved me. I was still living in a new home, in a new town trying to start a new life. Those things were the same. And yet, in a divine second, my heart recognized this Love, and then, rejection fled. Left in its place was a profound understanding of the immeasurable love Jesus had for me. I was *relished* by the King of Kings. The Creator of the Universe adored me. And if Jesus loves me, calls me by name, and reaches into a tiny apartment to remind me of this life changing truth, then really, what does it matter what anyone else thinks of me? I'm loved by Jesus!

This overwhelms me when I think of it. And my prayer is that you will see yourself, through the loving and adoring eyes of Jesus, and feel this in your soul. So deep that nothing can shake it again. I believe when we can fully understand the doting love of Jesus, accept His promise of Love, and turn to Him for reminders of our worth, we will experience life in the Valley of Rejection (and all valleys) with greater comfort.

> Rejection loses power when we hold it up to Jesus.

The pain does not necessarily end when we grasp this Love. But rejection loses its sting when viewed through the indescribable, unfathomable love of Jesus. Let me say it another way, rejection loses power when we hold it up to Jesus. His light is too bright, and His glory too great, to leave any room for rejection. In those moments and hours when the rejection story in our souls threatens to consume us, and we are overrun with heart wrenching thoughts of pain, we can count on Him and His Word to remind us of the Truth. We are not rejectable. In fact, being made as replicas of God Himself, we are designed and created uniquely and beautifully. His fingerprints are all over us. And He adores His creation. We are anything but rejectable.

We cannot replace the truth of God's opinion with the lies of someone else's words. His Truth stands.

A Miracle On Gladwin Street

Walking up to the church on Gladwin Street the first day was like a scene out of a homecoming event. From the distance I could feel the excitement. The intoxicating cheering and laughter brought a lightness to my heart that I had not felt in many months. Rounding the corner, my eyes found the source of this celebration—a large group of young people lined the sidewalks and filled the parking lot of the church. Some of them were waving to passing cars, while others held large signs above their heads that read, "Welcome to Church! You belong here!"

My heart raced as I worked my way up the long driveway to this huge church. Today was the first Sunday in my new home, my new community, and now, in my new church.

Leaving behind my family home the week prior was almost more than I thought I could bear. I had hustled for months to gain back the love that my husband no longer had for me. His shocking decision to leave the relationship left me desperate for understanding that I would never find. In an effort to touch a soft spot in him that might bring him back to our life and our God, I decided to cover Him in God's promises, leaving him countless notes and reminders that he was loved—loved by God and loved by me. I tucked notes in his clothes, in his car, and everywhere I thought he might look with the message, *You are loved. You are so loved.*

It felt like a hustle. It felt vulnerable. It felt desperate. And the lack of impact left me feeling even more confused and very unloved. Adding insult to my injury, my attempts to show him love all landed flat. He was unmoved by my words. Unmoved by my heartache. And in my desperation, I found myself forgetting one very important truth—I, too, am loved.

Nearing the driveway of the church, many of these cheering voices and waving flags turned my way. Heart still racing, I picked up my pace. Shame tried hard to derail me, insisting that my current marital status was evidence of my worthlessness. Anxiety stood by and jeered at me, taunting me to turn around. *You don't belong here*, my emotions told me in unison. *Everyone will see your scarlet letter. You should go home.*

Holding tight to my courage, I reminded myself out loud, "I belong to Jesus." Somewhere inside of me, I knew I belonged. These were my people, and I needed to be here. As I wrestled with the criticism and voices in my mind, a young man holding a huge sign turned to face me. Everything stood still in that moment.

I can still see his smile and the beautiful words he held, as he thrust the sign toward me, revealing the most beautiful message. "You are

> It felt like a holy hand from Heaven had just reached through that sign and wrapped His fingers around my heart.

loved." It felt like a holy hand from Heaven had just reached through that sign and wrapped His fingers around my heart. *You are loved. You are loved.* I felt my steps get lighter. In fact, I think I almost skipped up the rest of the driveway. I let God's truth drown out the lies of my emotions. *I am loved. I am loved.*

Seeing my brave, but ringless, hand reach toward the front door of this new church building reminded me of my alone-ness and my lost identity, I hesitated. Once again, shame tried to steal the truth. I had a choice to make, give in to the shame-based rejection story, or claim God's truth about me. I felt victory as I reached for the door again and walked inside.

It was name-tag Sunday. With shaking hands, I wrote my name on a tag, peeled the backing off, and stuck it to my chest. Taking a courageous deep breath, I looked up and found a multitude of friendly faces who began calling me by name. In an instant, this newly single, heartbroken and shame-filled woman, who was sure she bore a scarlet letter, became *Nicole*, loved and welcomed. And known by name.

Jesus pursues His kids. He holds sign after sign to remind us of His love, and He plants people and things along the way to be His hands and feet. Love is an action word, and God's Love in Action approach to pursuing His children is all around us. We walk broken-hearted through the valley, carrying the poisonous names rejection hands us. And with the touch of His hand, He reminds us we are wanted more than we can ever understand. We hold our breath, wincing from the shame-based story, insisting we hide away and cover up. But every single time, He breathes life, holds up signs, and lifts our heads.

He died for us. And He would do it again and again, just to have us. My friend, if I've learned anything in this valley, it's this: You can trust Him. If He says it, it's true. If He promises to do it, He will.

A Conversation I'd Love to Sit In On

> Perfect Love is the antidote for rejection.

Perfect Love is the antidote for rejection. The Creator of the universe stands beside you and calls you loved, wanted, and relished. The creator of the universe chooses *you*. He looks at you with love in His eyes. He listens when you speak and hurts when you hurt. He does not tire of your antics or think you're too much. He thinks about you and smiles. He gets that twinkle in His eye when He looks at you, full of love, overjoyed that you are His. He delights in you. Delights.

Think of this really beautiful scene for a moment. Jesus shows up and engages in a conversation with the person who has rejected you. It's an interesting image, isn't it? On your right, sits that person, and on the left, Jesus. He's leaning forward, arms propped casually on his legs, gentleness all over His face, wearing a smile. They're talking to each other while we watch.

The rejector says, "I'm done with her."

Jesus says, "*I will never be done with her. In fact, I can't get enough of her. I relish her.*"

The rejector says, "She's too much."

Jesus says, "*Too much what? That doesn't make sense to me. She's exactly how I made her.*"

The rejector says, "I want a different life."

Jesus says, *"I can't imagine a life without her."*

The rejector says, "I don't love her anymore."

Jesus says, *"I am going to love her unconditionally for the rest of eternity. The love I feel for her in this moment is actually too deep for her to fathom. I am overflowing with it. I literally died for her—I adore her so much. And I'd happily die for her again."*

Jesus is a Man of action. His love moves Him to do incredible things. That's the story of the cross, it's the story of His pursuit of you. And it's the story of how He is traveling with you through this valley. He is not afraid of your pain or uncomfortable with your emotions. He just loves. And it's this incredible love that prompts Him to rush to your side and provide His amazing rescue of you. Will you accept this Love? Will you turn toward the One Who is pursuing you and let Him love you? No matter what has happened to you, regardless of anything that someone else has said, there is a greater truth you need to know. You are *not* rejectable in the eyes of Jesus—you *are* relished!

KEY TAKEAWAYS

- Jesus relishes you. To relish means: adore, delight, find favour and enjoy immensely.

- Your current rejection story does not define your value and does not impact God's immeasurable love for you.

- God flips our shame stories on their heads, and He calls us necessary, chosen, beloved.

- Time alone with Jesus is the antidote for loneliness.

- Perfect Love is the antidote for rejection.

Zefaniah 3:17
Phillipians 1:6

REJECTION RECOVERY

See what great love the Father has lavished on us, that we should be called children of God! And that is what we are! (1 John 3:1a).

THERAPEUTIC QUESTIONS

- What gets in the way of you fully experiencing and understanding the unfathomable love of Jesus?

- How would life be different if you could accept this Love and see yourself through the eyes of Jesus?

- In what ways might Jesus be trying to tell you He loves you?

- What might help you be more open to this unconditional love He is offering you?

JOURNAL PROMPT

Write the above scripture in your journal. Highlight, underline, and circle the words that jump out at you. Read the key words out loud. How do you feel?

Dear Jesus, I know the Bible says You love me. But I am struggling to really understand the fullness of what that means. Please help me accept Your love, God. Heal the broken parts that get in the way of accepting your love for me. And help me to break the thinking and feeling that get in the way of understanding You better. Please help me to trust Your love and Your loyalty to me. Thank you for standing with me through this valley. Amen.

CHAPTER 7

Rescued

"The paradox is this: if we never need rescuing, we'll never know the Rescuer."

—Beth Moore

Brokenness is a breeding ground for anxiety. The newly formed path I was creating around my coffee table evidenced this exhausting truth. I knew what was happening. I recognized the frantic feeling that makes us want to crawl out of our skin. The racing thoughts and the heaviness on my chest were familiar—panic was building, and I was desperate for an intervention.

I needed to pray but the words were gone. I wanted to read the Bible and fill my mind with the soothing promises of my Heavenly Father, but the tears flooding my face were uncontrolled and messy.

In desperation, I sank to the floor, opened my Bible, and—wait for it—I dropped it on my face. Yep, you read that right. Splayed out like a starfish on the floor of my living room, I lay there, Bible on my face, in a full out panic attack.

It was an ugly-cry situation. I let myself go into an all-out, desperate, snotty nose, can't breathe kind of sob. I laid there with my face planted in Amos, completely devastated, and overwhelmed with questions. *Why God? Why did this happen?* With determined conviction, I took a long, slow, deep breath in. Peace, there it was, at the end of myself.

This storm had leveled me and left me pleading with Jesus to reach through His pages, wrap His arms around my broken heart, and make it better. In that moment, it was just me and God. I leaned in and He held on. I told Him through the desperate cries of my heart how lost I felt and how broken I was. True to character, He reminded me I was not alone in my pain. My cries to Him, my dependence on Him, was exactly what He wanted.

> God is never closer than when His child is hurting.

God is never closer than when His child is hurting. We run wide-eyed and frantic through valleys of life, and there He is, leaned in, elbows on knees, hands open in front of Him, waiting for us to look to Him for help. And when we remember to look to Him and take our eyes off the waves of the storm or the darkness of the valley, He rushes in to comfort His child. Sometimes He heals and sometimes He holds, but our pain is always His call to action.

> Your valley, regardless of its size, is not bigger than our God. Your season of suffering does not trump His authority.

Your valley, regardless of its size, is not bigger than our God. Your season of suffering does not trump His authority. There is nothing we face that has not passed by the watchful eyes of our Heavenly Father. And as we lean hard on Him and trust Him to navigate us through, we will find relief in His sovereignty and see His fingerprints on the details.

The Why Question

My field research in the valley of rejection had me asking why. *Why would God allow this? Why did He not answer my prayers to heal my husband's heart and bring him home?*

Have you been there before, asking the *why* question? Wondering if you will ever find the purpose in your pain or enjoy some level of understanding? God is not afraid of our questions. He doesn't shake His head at us or roll His eyes. As I write this there are still many unanswered questions about that time of my life. But the answer I did receive not only surprised me, it also changed my life. And while there is still mystery in what I'm about to say, the rejection I experienced was actually a divine rescue in disguise.

This may not be the same truth for you. Our stories and experiences are different, but even in the differences, the truth remains—rescues are one of God's greatest specialties.

The Bible is bursting with examples reminding us that God is heavily invested in the lives of His kids. He doesn't leave us to face our pain alone. In fact, He moves in, pulls us out of things not meant for us, and leads us in the direction He calls us to. God goes and gets His kids. His love prompts Him to action. And when His children head in a direction outside of His will, He designs a rescue.

And not just a rescue *from* something, but a rescue *for* something.

The Cross was the ultimate rescue. When God gave up His Son, we needed a divine intervention. And Jesus was the only Way. He provided our escape from death and our rescue for life. It wasn't enough for Him to just save us from something, He saves us with the intended purpose of giving us eternal life.

> This is the greatest thing about being rescued by God—His rescue holds a dual purpose.

This is the greatest thing about being rescued by God—His rescue holds a dual purpose. You were rescued both *from* and *for* something. And it communicates a very important message to us: we are loved and valued by Him.

Rescues by their very nature are rooted in two principles:

1. A rescue is a response to distress.
2. Being rescued proves value. By nature, a rescue is a declaration of worth. If it's not valuable, it's not worth saving.

Come with me for a moment to my hometown on the glorious shores of Georgian Bay, an enormous body of water connected to Lake Huron in Ontario, Canada. As is common on the Great Lakes, winds blow in, and while the kite surfers rush to take advantage of the waves, the rest of us frantically collect our water loungers and make way for cover. During one particular windstorm, I had an important decision to make. My pool noodle, with surprising determination, lifted off the patio, landed in the waves and began a rapid escape into open water. At the same time, my paddleboard teetered and then launched forcefully in the opposite direction. The dilemma? Save the paddleboard or save the noodle?

You know how this story goes. Of course, I let the noodle go and swam after my board. Why? Because of its value and worth. Now, I am very new to paddleboarding. And by new, I mean I'm bad at it. I lack the grace and finesse required to master such an activity. So, the rescue of the paddleboard was not pretty. Seeing me crawling up on that thing must have been quite a sight. Finding a stable standing position then turning it around to bring it home, required the stuff of reality television shows. After wrestling with the board, we both came home bruised and battle weary.

What if rejection is actually a divine, albeit painful, and messy rescue? What if there is purpose in the pain, and this is God's way of bringing you home, closer to Him, and more in line with what He has planned for you?

And, what if we choose to see our suffering, not as undeserved acts against us, but as part of God's sovereign plan *for* us? His larger plan exceeds our limited capacity to understand our circumstances. The pain-filled valley of rejection consumes us at first. But when we allow ourselves to view it through an eternal lens, we find it less overwhelming.

Gaining that heavenly perspective gives us some insight into the possibility that this rejection is a divine rescue. An ordained repositioning meant to bring you closer to your Heavenly Father.

> What if we choose to see our suffering, not as undeserved acts against us, but as part of God's sovereign plan for us?

A Divine Repositioning

When God ordains a rescue of His child, He does not do it off the side of His desk. Our intervention is carefully orchestrated because He loves us too much to leave us heading in the wrong direction. Every rescue holds purpose, and woven within each are uniquely customized elements of connection, protection, and correction.

Reflect back over your season in the valley. Can you see how your rescue brought you closer to Jesus? Have you been talking with Him more, leaning harder on Him, becoming aware of His presence in ways you hadn't been? There's the connection. God desires intimacy with us, and He is a jealous Father. He's not afraid to scoop us up out of the things that take us away from Him.

> God desires intimacy with us, and He is a jealous Father. He's not afraid to scoop us up out of the things that take us away from Him.

If you take a long look at the situation surrounding your rejection, can you see areas where you needed protection? What is God protecting you from? And what about correction? Many rescues hold very obvious elements of correction—God disciplines those He loves.

And finally, there's one more important thing to keep in mind. Our purpose on this planet is to bring glory to Jesus. Since God created us to bring Him glory, our rescue holds the purpose of promoting Jesus. The intervention, disguised as rejection, was divinely orchestrated as a means to draw us closer to Him, protect us and correct us, and ultimately to bring glory to God and reach others with our story.

But we cannot be passive bystanders in this process. If we are to experience all that God wants to offer us through His rescue, we must take on a posture of obedience and a willingness to trust Him and follow Him through the valley. Trusting Jesus to complete this rescue and bring us through the valley safely, is an act of our will and an opportunity to grow our faith, leaving room for a lifesaving miracle.

Let's decide today to accept the rescue. It's a decision you will not regret, and as you find yourself continually nurtured and loved by our Heavenly Father, the struggle eases and you will begin to see this valley as a beautiful place of renewal.

KEY TAKEAWAYS

- We are rescued from something and for something.

- Our ultimate purpose is to bring glory to God, this rescue will help point others toward Him.

- A rescue is a response to distress.

- Rescues are faith building.

- The Ultimate rescue was Jesus, sent to die for us.

- Rejection may be a rescue in disguise.

REJECTION RECOVERY

The Lord says, "I will rescue those who love me. I will protect those who trust in my name. When they call on me, I will answer; I will be with them in trouble. I will rescue and honor them" (Psalm 91:14-15 NLT).

THERAPEUTIC QUESTIONS

- How would life feel and look differently if you believed you have been rescued?

- If rejection is a divine rescue, what might it be a rescue from? What might you be rescued for?

- What stands in the way of a full rescue by God? What things are acting as obstacles in the way of accepting this rescue?

- If this is a rescue from some self-defeating behaviours, beliefs, or personality traits that God is trying to bring you away from, what might they be?

JOURNAL PROMPT

One day I'm going to tell the story of this messy rescue. What is the story I want to be able to tell?

Dear Jesus, thank you for rescuing me. It's been messy and painful, and to be honest, it hasn't felt like much of a rescue yet. I want to trust You and believe You have this all figured out. Please help my unbelief. Help me to turn to You when the water gets higher and the heat of the fire gets hotter. I accept Your rescue and trust You to bring me out of this pain and lead me toward what You have for me on the other side. Amen.

CHAPTER 8

Redeemed

"The same gentle hands that hold me when I'm broken, they conquer death to bring me victory."

—NICOLE C. MULLEN

It kind of just happened. I lost my grip, things were in the way, and when the pot came down, it came down hard. Into many dusty, jagged pieces with a cringeworthy sound, this beautiful ceramic favourite found its fate on my garage floor. I stood in silent horror, my eyes fixed on the brokenness. Anger galloped to the scene, as I scoured the garage for something or someone to blame. Tears of frustration and sadness began to flow down my face. This pot held special memories for me and bending to pick up the pieces felt like an unwelcome ending to a season I cherished.

If you love plants like I do, you will understand my emotional attachment to this clay pot. It had been the perfect summer planter over the years. It held beautiful flowering greenery welcoming guests and bringing me much joy. And on this day, pulling the garbage can closer, I grumbled aloud how sorry I was that it's time had come to an end. "What good is a broken pot?" I asked.

Kneeling amongst those jagged pieces of broken pottery, I felt a nudge from Heaven. With clarity only my Heavenly Father can give, I began to see myself in the messiness of this situation. As I've fallen off ledges, crashed hard to the valley floor, and left pieces of myself in life choices, my brokenness has sometimes left me feeling useless to Jesus. I've wondered how He could make something beautiful come from the fragments and splinters of my life.

But God is brilliant at redeeming broken things. He is the ultimate Potter, with a flare and creativity that leave us in awe of His handiwork. He loves picking up the broken bits of His kids and making something new.

The Bible is full of broken pots. I love the redemption stories of Ruth and Naomi, and the woman at the well. And I'm drawn to Jesus' special attention to Peter, His friend who betrayed Him. With grace, Jesus brought Peter's shame to an end and used him for incredible things. Or Paul, formerly a murderer, and then one of the most important instruments for God's work. David committed adultery, had a man murdered to cover it up, and then still, God in His mercy showed generous grace and used this broken pot.

A renewed sense of hope consumed my sadness that day on the garage floor. God reminded me that beautiful things can come from brokenness. I went to work on repurposing and restoring my pot. I sorted through the shards, pulling out the larger pieces and cleaning off the dusty, jagged parts. Some were perfect for the new role I had chosen, others needed to be broken down further. I wanted all of them—every fragment was necessary to complete the project I had in mind.

For several weeks I carefully and intentionally repurposed my favourite pot, by pairing it with an old mirror. Broken bit by broken bit, I created a beautiful mosaic frame. The shattered splinters of my pot formed a beautiful pattern around the glass, and the colours popped in ways I had never noticed before.

Delighted with my new mirror, I hung it in my office, where for many years it framed the courageous faces of the women who came and went from my space. Perhaps more than that, it prompted countless conversations about how beauty is often unleashed through brokenness. And how the road to redemption is a journey of sharp edges and broken bits.

New and Greatly Improved

If I'm honest, writing about redemption has forced me elbow deep in research. Thank you to C.S. Lewis for helping me unmuddy the waters to understand this divine repurposing. In his book, *Mere Christianity*, Lewis says, "For mere improvement is not redemption, though redemption always improves people even here and now and will, in the end, improve them to a degree we cannot yet imagine. God became man to turn creatures into sons: not simply to produce better men of the old kind but to produce a new kind of man."[4]

> To be redeemed is to be delivered, set free, and made new.

Redemption is not simply becoming a better version of ourselves. It's a total overhauling, a divine reconstruction. To be redeemed is to be delivered, set free, and made new. Redemption holds many benefits:

- Peace - *"For God was pleased to have all his fullness dwell in him, and through him to reconcile to himself all things, whether things on earth or things in heaven, by making peace through his blood, shed on the cross"* (Colossians 1:19–20).

- Adoption into God's family - *"But when the time set had fully come, God sent his Son, born of a woman, born under the law, to redeem those under the law, that we might receive adoption to sonship"* (Galatians 4:4–5).

- Forgiveness - *"In him we have redemption through his blood, the forgiveness of sins, in accordance with the riches of God's grace"* (Ephesians 1:7).

- Freedom - *"Christ redeemed us from the curse of the law by becoming a curse for us, for it is written: 'Cursed is everyone who is hung on a pole.' He redeemed us in order that the blessing given to Abraham might come to the Gentiles through Christ Jesus, so that by faith we might receive the promise of the Spirit"* (Galatians 3:13).

- Eternal life - *"For God so loved the world that he gave his one and only Son, that whoever believes in him shall not perish but have eternal life"* (John 3:16).

God is in the business of redemption and restoration. In His creative, nurturing hands, our broken bits and pieces are woven together into customized masterpieces. Our Heavenly Father has a vision for His children. Your purpose on this earth is not extinguished by the wipeouts and face plants you've experienced. In fact, it's the messy bits and pieces we wish away that hold the most promise for His vision.

> God is in the business of redemption and restoration.

It doesn't matter how far you've gone or how broken you feel. God is in passionate pursuit of you. His all-out, radical devotion to His children propels Him into action and draws Him into a tireless chase through the hills and valleys of our lives. The purpose of His pursuit is to actively include us in His redemptive work and restore us back to who we were meant to be, who He created us to be.

Redemption is God choosing and pursuing us. It happens in an instant and requires nothing from us. When we trust Him and turn to Him in our brokenness, He will absolutely make good on His promise to bring us through this pain. Three incredibly important things happen when Jesus redeems us.

We are no longer hostages of our past or slaves to sin. Rather, we belong in God's kingdom. He calls us His and we are celebrated members of His family.

We are forgiven of sins and will not experience the penalty of sin. This includes the removal of guilt and shame we feel because of the things we have done.

We are returned to the original position God intended for us. Redemption brings us back into the fold, exactly as God had originally designed it.

A Three Step Process

> While redemption is God pursuing us, restoration is us reciprocating that pursuit and continually deciding to choose Jesus.

Restoration is not the same as redemption. While redemption is God pursuing us, restoration is us reciprocating that pursuit and continually deciding to choose Jesus. We don't drift into restoration; we choose it intentionally. We deny the things that take us away from the process of restoration and turn wholeheartedly back, time and time again, in the direction of Jesus. He wants to be the Saviour of our soul, and He wants to be the Leader of our lives. Restoration, just like redemption, isn't something to be earned. It's something we surrender to. Losing sight of this important distinction leaves us feeling like failures, because we think we should be changed immediately. But restoration is a lifestyle, a process, focused on surrendering daily to God's will.

God's plan is to make all things new. His vision for your life is as unique as you are and through this redemption process, He is asking you to agree with Him about your worth and your purpose. To partner with God in the restoration process we need to:

1. *Remember the past, but don't live in it.*

    Remembering how God healed us and how He showed up for us helps us appreciate grace and keeps us involved in the restoration process. From this view we can hold the past as an informant, not as a place to revisit.

2. *Consistently connect with God.*

    God did His part by redeeming us through the death of Jesus on the cross. The restoration process involves a daily decision to connect intentionally with God, making time with Him a priority.

3. *Live with the end in mind.*

    Our performance does not impact God's opinion of us. God is just getting started in our lives. Restoration can be a difficult and painful process—but this pain is purposeful. The process of healing requires us to endure some discomfort along the way as we build resilience and readiness for the plan God has for us. Keep your eye on the prize. Healing is coming.

We are not broken pots any more. While there is a history of brokenness and the raw spots still exist, God has not left us undone or unfinished. His divine repurposing plan for your life is in full swing, and the jagged edges you are worried about are going to be showstoppers in the new mosaic He is creating in you. Wait for it—His redeeming work is going to bring you through this valley with a story worth telling and a restoration testimony that will bring hope to those still in pieces.

KEY TAKEAWAYS

- God uses broken things all the time. He is the Master Potter.

- You are never too far gone to be outside of His love and His desire to redeem your story.

- Broken things make beautiful mosaics.

- God's practice is to bring beauty from ashes. His redeeming grace means our past can be used for ministry.

- Redemption is God choosing us. Restoration is us continually choosing God.

- Redemption happens in an instant—restoration is a lifelong process.

- Your passions + Your gifts + Your experiences = Your ministry.

Collations: 113
Roman: 8:38
John: 14:17
Roman: 12:2

REJECTION RECOVERY

This means that anyone who belongs to Christ has become a new person. The old life is gone; a new life has begun! (2 Corinthians 5:17 NLT).

THERAPEUTIC QUESTIONS

- If you invited rejection and redemption to the same party, what would redemption have to say to rejection?

- What does redemption feel like?

- When rejection pushes back against the story of redemption, what will help put it back in its place?

- Can you foresee life without rejection? From that vantage point, what did it take to leave rejection behind and embrace the freedom of redemption?

JOURNAL PROMPT

If it's been permitted, it has purpose. And if it has purpose, it holds promise. What does this mean to you?

Dear Jesus, you came to earth to die for me. I don't deserve your love or this redemption, but You offered it freely. Your pursuit of me and your determination to bring me home is amazing to me. Thank you for pursuing me like You have and for buying me back, for redeeming me. I want to stay in Your plans for my life. Please give me the wisdom to stay close to you. Amen.

CHAPTER 9

Released

"We are products of our past, but we don't have to be prisoners of it."

—RICK WARREN

Enormous steel doors slammed behind us, as we walked through the courtyard and toward the final gate, signifying her freedom. A duffel bag tossed over her shoulder contained everything she owned. Her slip-on plastic sandals would have to do until we could find a thrift shop to pick up some new ones. Twelve years had passed since Wendy walked free, and her posture on this day was not as one would expect for a woman just released from jail.

With the mountain of official paperwork behind us, she had said her goodbyes—but these last steps to freedom halted her in her tracks. With fear and sadness in her eyes, she looked straight at me and said, "I can't do it. I can't go out there. I don't want to stay here, but I don't know how to be free."

I had known Wendy for four years. Our first meetings were through the meal slot of her isolation cell, with guards standing on each side of the door. Protocol for these meetings meant I had to position my chair off to the side of that tiny, rectangular opening to avoid any unforeseen body fluids that might come my way. Wendy was instructed to sit on the floor in her cell without movement, where she was visible for the guards watching her on camera.

We met like this a few times a week for about a month, until I petitioned the administration to allow us to meet face to face. Other than Wendy's mugshot, I really had no idea what she looked like. Eager to do our visits in person, without a steel door between us, I felt grateful when I received the message, *Permission granted.*

On the day of our first face-to-face meeting, an enthusiastic smile lit up the concrete room as Wendy shuffled enthusiastically toward the table where I was waiting for her. She was shackled and handcuffed, but her words of gratitude flowed freely. "Thank you for getting me out of there," she said with a sincere smile.

"It's my pleasure to meet you," I replied. And it was. I was delighted to have Wendy here, where the necessary connection needed for her healing work could begin.

For three more years, Wendy and I met weekly. During that time, Wendy's good behaviour earned her release out of isolation and allowed her back onto the regular unit with the other inmates. It was a tremendous challenge and an incredible honour to work with this woman, to watch her grow, learn, and heal from the wounds of her past. I only hoped her progress would continue.

Wendy had experienced many releases in her life. As a child, she was taken from her parents and placed in foster care where she spent most of her childhood trying to stay safe from abusive adults. She was physically and sexually abused daily, and she began to act out against authority, resulting in punishment she could never bring herself to describe out loud.

When she was finally returned to her family, everything was different. Over the next ten years, Wendy's pain led her into activities and behaviours that landed her in several detention centres. She eventually ended up with a long-term sentence in a federal correctional facility. She was living with severe mental health and addiction issues, and she was estranged from most of her family, except a special friend from her community who she called Sweet Aunt Rosie.

On this day, Wendy's release from the federal jail she had called home for more than a decade meant change. From my perspective, Wendy was being released *from* something unfavourable: jail. But she was also being released *to* something positive: freedom.

We worked tirelessly on her release plan, arranged housing, identification, even employment in a community of her choice. For almost a year, Wendy had her sights set on this day. She was not shy about the countdown, announcing enthusiastically to anyone who would listen, "One hundred seventy-six days until I get to go home."

It became an ongoing conversation between Wendy and the staff—everyone knew she was being released in X number of days. She had her first *freedom meal* planned: a Big Mac and fries. "Extra fries, please." She talked regularly about how fresh the air would smell and how much louder the birds would chirp on the other side of that gate.

As the lead clinician, I had pulled together a caring team of professionals to assist with Wendy's release plan, who would help ensure her move to the new town would occur as seamlessly as possible. The team on the other end of this complex arrangement was ready to receive Wendy. They had been actively involved and were eager to help her reintegrate into the community upon her release. My overnight bags were packed, the fleet vehicles were fueled up, and everyone was ready for Wendy's release. Everyone, except Wendy.

Wendy had become comfortable with her life on the inside. She developed relationships with other offenders, who now felt like family. She knew what was expected of her, and she knew how to move in the system. Through many years of heartache leading to life choices that hurt her, Wendy found herself in a life nowhere near what she had dreamt as a little girl.

In one of our sessions, I asked Wendy to tell me about her younger self. Animated and emotional, Wendy described happy memories with her parents and her brothers. She shared her love of music, the ocean, and the dream of being a mother and a teacher. "But not just any teacher," she said, "I wanted to be the teacher that everyone remembers as their favourite!"

On her release day, that childhood dream was long gone, and Wendy was scared. She didn't think she could manage freedom, and she doubted she deserved it. During one of our last sessions, Wendy looked up at me with tears in her eyes and whispered words I will never forget, "I don't think women like me get to walk free."

Standing on the edge of freedom that day, I knew Wendy's mind was running with this message. Fear had crept in, shame was running amuck, and Wendy was paralyzed. I stood there with car keys in hand, looking at a woman who had travelled a painfully hard road, but now could not accept what was being offered to her. For fear? Because of doubt? Disbelief?

I put my arm around Wendy's shoulder. I reminded her that everything was prepared for her. She had served her time, and the plan was in motion for her success. I had hoped this day would bring celebration. I thought freedom was a good thing. Wendy just needed to take the step. Ahead of her was freedom. She was released.

Accepting Freedom—Wrestling with Shame

But what if freedom is daunting and being released brings fear? How do we live outside of the familiar? What do we do if we don't want to stay in the past, but we can't imagine a different future? And what if the normal we are accustomed to, detains us more than frees us?

I don't know about you, but I understand why accepting freedom and allowing ourselves release is so hard. Guilt and shame travel with us through our valleys. And whether we like it or not, they become familiar companions. Anxiety piggybacks on insecurity, and together this assault team declares us unworthy of freedom and incapable of managing it. We become hostages to our past, holding onto hurts and maintaining habits that bring greater levels of pain. When pain informs our choices, it takes us through a spin cycle of self-defeating, jagged-edged suffering which inevitably keeps us from ever experiencing release. But God in His Word takes a hard stand against our human propensity to stay stuck in the past.

> When pain informs our choices, it takes us through a spin cycle of self-defeating, jagged-edged suffering which inevitably keeps us from ever experiencing release.

The Bible says in Galatians 5:1, *"For freedom Christ has set us free; stand firm therefore, and do not submit again to the yoke of slavery"* (ESV). And Jesus tells us in John 8:36, *"So if the Son sets you free you are truly free"* (NLT). The message is clear, God's heart is that we would rest in the freedom He has offered, let the past go, and find peace in His good plans for our lives. This release means we get to sit on the cusp on a new start, a new adventure.

> God's heart is that we would rest in the freedom He has offered, let the past go, and find peace in His good plans for our lives.

The old is gone. And as we gaze ahead toward the future, we can trust our Heavenly Father to keep His eyes on us as we travel. If God is calling us forward, if He points His finger in our direction and beckons us toward Him, we can absolutely trust Him to travel this release plan with us.

Non-smokers Don't Smoke

Releasing the past and accepting freedom is not a passive experience. I will never forget the moment I felt the shift. It started with a decision. Letting go of the past requires us to decide we are done with holding on to it. While this may be obvious, it's certainly not easy. When we decide the past no longer serves us, that it is in fact, holding us back from experiencing all that God has for us, we can begin to release our grip on all we have been carrying.

Olivia came to counseling in January as part of her self-care strategy for the year, determined to make this season a pivot point in her life. She wanted to leave behind who she no longer wanted to be and turn boldly toward her best self. To this end, she put down things that didn't serve her anymore and picked up things she decided were in line with who she wanted to be. A smoker for almost twenty years, Olivia said she had a love-hate relationship with cigarettes. After a *breakup with cigarettes* ceremony, she released herself from the identity of *smoker*, and picked up the identity of *nonsmoker*. How did she do this? She made a decision to live as a nonsmoker. That very conscious decision released her from an identity she no longer wanted and a connection to something she no longer wanted to carry.

I was curious about this. It seemed too simple. Very matter-of-factly, Olivia explained, "Nonsmokers don't smoke." And just like that, she was done.

While it might not be that easy for everyone, the principle fits here. Living free requires a decision to let go of what doesn't serve us and to pick up a new identity. Released. If I have been set free, why would I live a life of captivity? Freed people live like it. So how do we do this?

Living as free people, released from the past and unencumbered to experience what God has for us, is an act of obedience. Release requires us to make a decision and act on it with Olivia's matter of fact determination. Working this through myself, and then with clients, I found the process of releasing and accepting freedom easier with the help of some therapeutic steps.

1. Get it all out and make it all right. This is the push and pull of emptying the past out onto the table, placing all of the bits and pieces in front of God, and asking Him to have a look. Are there things in the past you need to tell Him about? Secrets you hold, pain you carry, or thoughts about Him, yourself, or others you have been afraid to address? This is your chance. Share your feelings, all of them. Get right with Him and let yourself enjoy the peace this refreshed relationship brings. Do you need to ask Him for forgiveness? Are there shame-based stories holding you hostage in the hurt? Do you struggle with pride, anger, anxiety? I did, and I think many of us do. Get it out. Tell Him everything. Everything! He can handle it. And His eyes won't roll in frustration. He won't shake His head at you or turn away. There will be no groans of exasperation. No sarcasm. And no walking away. What you will find is His face, full of love and compassion. His eyes shining with joy. And His arms open so wide and so ready to bring you home.

2. Forgive. This part of the release plan is a sticking point for many of us, isn't it? For many years the word forgiveness felt like a slap in the face for me. How could I forgive such betrayal? How could I ever be okay with what happened,

what was said, what's been done? And forgiving not just what was done to me, but also what had been taken from me—forgiving what was taken from my daughter. Well, I just didn't know how. This unbelievable struggle with forgiveness helped me address the myths that may keep some of us from even beginning to try. Do any of these statements sound familiar?

Myth #1	Forgiveness condones the action of the person who harmed us.
Myth #2	Forgiveness must lead to reconciliation with the person who harmed us.
Myth #3	Forgiveness will send the message that they were right to do what they did.
Myth #4	Forgiveness will make me seem/feel weak or set me up for further hurt.
Myth #5	Forgiveness means I have to forget the behaviour.
Myth #6	Forgiveness is a gift or favour to the other person.

The truth is, forgiveness is something completely separate from the other person. It's an agreement between you and God. It does not condone or agree with what the other person did, nor does it require us to be in relationship with them or forget how they hurt us. Forgiveness is an act of obedience and is necessary for *your* release plan.

And what about self-forgiveness? What about the harmful, hurtful things we have done and said that have been less than honouring to God? Sometimes self-forgiveness is even more difficult than forgiving others. The Bible reminds us in 2 Corinthians 5:17, *"This means that anyone who belongs to Christ has become a new person. The old life is gone; a new life has begun!"* (NLT).

To not forgive ourselves is to disagree with God that His Son's death on the cross was enough. To hold shame and guilt means we think God is wrong. Let's let that linger a bit. The death of Jesus for our sins on the cross means we are forgiven and set free. The Ultimate release plan was put in place over 2,000 years ago, and you and I were on His mind when He hung on that cross. We are forgiven. God wasn't wrong. We are free.

3. Accept the gift of freedom and decide on an attitude of excitement and gratitude. Grace is a gift we don't deserve. So, let's stop trying to push it away because we don't think we deserve it. You and I are both right, we don't deserve grace. But right now, you are being offered the greatest gift ever given—face the future arm-in-arm with the King of Kings. You can't earn it, and He doesn't want you to try. Just say yes. And, let's take this a step further, remember we're free. Free! This is worthy of celebration and a deep-rooted, heartfelt expression of gratitude. God did this for us. He has released us from the past and He has released us to an incredible future with Him.

> Living free and working our release plans require both a letting go and a falling forward.

Living free and working our release plans require both a letting go and a falling forward. Will you accept this gift with me? Let's link arms and stand with the King of Kings as He leads us away from the past and into this gift of freedom He has prepared for us.

KEY TAKEAWAYS

- God has set me free.

- Our release has two parts: We are released *from* something, and we are released *for* something.

- Free women do not live as hostages to their past.

- Living free is a decision rooted in trust that God is in control.

- Forgiveness requires us to be actively involved in walking away from holding others and ourselves hostage to mistakes.

- Releasing the past and accepting freedom is not a passive experience. It doesn't just happen. It requires a decision on our parts to let go of the harmful things we are holding onto and fall forward into God's plan for us.

REJECTION RECOVERY

> *Forget the former things; do not dwell on the past. See, I am doing a new thing! Now it springs up; do you not perceive it? I am making a way in the wilderness and streams in the wasteland (Isaiah 43:18-19).*

THERAPEUTIC QUESTIONS & ACTIVITY

- What stands in the way of your freedom?

- If you are being released, what else might you need release from? And what might you be released for?

- Write a letter. For me, I wrote a letter to my husband. It wasn't an angry letter, but rather a letting go letter, offering my forgiveness and grace. In my case, I sent it to him, but that isn't always my suggestion. You know best whether or not to send the letter, but there is therapeutic value in writing one. This is not an easy step, but it may provide closure and important movement in your healing.

JOURNAL PROMPT

To fully embrace freedom, release the past and accept who God is calling you to be. What are the top five things you feel you need to work through?

Heavenly Father, thank you for sending Jesus to die for my release. I struggle to let go of the things that have hurt me and the things I've done that are keeping me from really experiencing the freedom You have for me. Can you help me with this? I want to move forward in Your plan, and I want to trust You in all areas of my life. Please give me understanding and help me let go of what is keeping me from all You have for me. Release me from the pain that holds me back. Heal me and help me forgive what's been done to me. I agree with you that Jesus' death was enough. Amen.

CHAPTER 10

Remember

"Be grateful for the wound that pushes you toward God."

—Yasmin Mogahed

The Valley makes us hungry. It's the place we devour self-help information, Scripture, encouragement, and healing input with urgency. It can turn us from passive participants in the nosebleed section of life, to front row, getting our hands dirty, active contenders for relief. Every second in the valley demands our attention.

And then one morning the valley seems less dark, less daunting, smoother. It's as though we turn a corner, and the jagged obstacles that have tripped us up and left us bruised begin to fade into the past. Valley living is like this, isn't it? The front end is sharp, grief is intense, and every step requires determination to keep moving. And then we start to notice the once jagged edges of grief begin to feel softer, the anxiety quiets a bit, and the once painfully slow moment-by-moment living feels more manageable.

With the steepest, darkest part of the valley in the rearview mirror, we get to enjoy some freedom from the pain. This is not to say the pain is over. Each of us travels the valley differently, so this may be many months post-rejection, or it may be just a few weeks. Your journey is unique and cannot be compared to anyone else's process.

However long it took you to get to this section of the valley, there is relief in this place.

Rejection leaves a sore spot in our hearts. It's unforgettable, really. And while we may be enjoying the fresh air of this smooth section of the valley, we can usually quite easily tap into the rawness of the loss. This pain is not something we easily forget.

Probably not surprising to you, women are hardwired to remember what we feel. We link feelings to almost everything, and memories are no different. This is both a beautiful thing and a tragic thing, all at the same time.

By the time this word *Remember* showed up for me, I had travelled through the valley of rejection. I was enjoying the sun on my face and freedom from pain that this part of the journey had to offer. I held a new understanding of God's incredible love and acceptance, and I was viewing myself through His lens. I no longer allowed the human lens to threaten and steal my identity. I knew I had been rescued *from* something God did not want for me, and I believed He had rescued me *for* something. I had been redeemed and released from the shame of my past. And now, with the valley of rejection behind me, I felt free.

> And now, with the valley of rejection behind me, I felt free.

This is what life outside of the valley feels like. It feels free. Galatians 5:1 says, "*So Christ has truly set us free. Now make sure that you stay free, and don't get tied up again in slavery to the law*" (NLT). Paul's letter to the Galatians here is meant to challenge them to walk in the truth they have learned about Jesus, to hold onto the freedom He presents, and to live in that freedom. For the Galatians, they were very caught up in the religiosity of the time, working to earn their freedom and believing that they could somehow gain God's favour by their works. The only reason we are free is because of the gift of Jesus. We don't make ourselves free. I did not make myself free, and you did not make yourself free. If you are standing on the pleasant side of the valley, Jesus did that for you. You are free because He brought you through.

Losing sight of this truth is easy. As humans we easily revert back to old patterns, even justifying these behaviours or deciding that simply dipping our toe in something won't lead us down a dark path. After all, we aren't stupid. We have learned our lessons in the valley, right?

Well, not me. I'm a slow learner. I started to notice that my devotional life slowed down, and I was spending less time in prayer. I added an '80s playlist to my Spotify account, and I was enjoying the walk down memory lane on my way to work, playing less worship music. And my thought life had turned to more worldly things, like shopping and scrolling through social media. Now, please don't read what I'm not writing here. Listening to '80s music, shopping, and some time on social media is not the problem. The problem was that I was forgetting to remember what I had learned in the valley. And worse, I was not adequately remembering Who rescued me and brought me through.

If History Teaches Us Anything

Just a few minutes in the book of Judges gives us a really good sense of what happens when we forget to remember. The Israelites, God's chosen people, had been on the receiving end of His incredible love for them. Through that love, God had rescued them time and time again, delivering them from a life of slavery, and leading them to the Promised Land. They had been redeemed, forgiven, and set free. And like rebellious children, they did not remember the cautionary command: *Honour God, follow His direction, and do right in the eyes of the Lord.*

It seems so obvious, doesn't it? All right, here is a confession. Until just recently, I have always read Judges with my nose in the air. Maybe even with a bit of a headshake and eye roll. And then, like He does, with firm gentleness, God reminded me that I am like Israel. I accept His love and His rescue. I cling to Him when He reaches in and saves me. I keep my eyes focused on Him while we travel the valley, wander in the desert, and weather the storm. And then, like foolish Israel, when I get to the other side, I dust myself off, fix my hair, take my eyes off of the Giver of this incredible gift of freedom, and do my own thing.

> There are people who need your words. They need to hear what God has done for you, and how He led you through the pain of rejection.

I can't stress this enough—remember to stay on track with Jesus. The valley you have been travelling through holds potential for ministry, and it must be used to show the love and grace of our Heavenly Father. There are people who need your words. They need to hear what God has done for you, and how He led you through the pain of rejection. There are people who have faced a loss similar to yours who can't imagine life on the other side of the valley. They are overwhelmed with anxiety and unable to breathe. Just like us, they need to know there is Hope, to be reminded that Jesus will not fail them. Your mess holds ministry, and the people God will bring into your life when you say *yes* to Him, are going to be healed and restored because of the things you remember from your time in the valley.

Things to Remember

Remember the Giver of the Gifts: When we find ourselves on the other side of the valley, it's easy to become less connected to the One Who rescued us. This is the place He brings us to so we can be more effective in ministry. It's here we need to lean hard on Him in a different way—not so much for a rescue, but for a repurposing. What do you want me to do now God?

Remember what He has brought you through: This is not to suggest ruminating on the pain and loss. Remember the valley as a season of your life when you needed to be reminded of your worth, your identity, and your needing of a rescue. It's a big deal what God has brought you through, and He deserves the credit for it.

Remember what you have learned: This is essential for the unique ministry God has for you. Others will want to know what you learned about yourself, about God, and about living through heartbreak. Focus on the lessons and miracles God did for you in the valley. This is your testimony, and there isn't another one like it.

Remember to forgive: This is a process—your wounds are deep. You have travelled a terribly hard road to get here. Spend time regularly giving over the pain and those who have harmed you to Jesus.

Forgiving does not communicate agreement, acceptance of an injustice, or require reconciliation. And it does not mean the pain goes away. It simply means you will no longer be limited or stunted by the wrong done to you. And this freedom makes room for healing.

Remember to forget: We know the spin cycle of pain we've struggled with in the past. Sometimes nasty narratives creep in, even on the tail end of the valley. It's time to let them go. This part of the valley requires us to stop spinning on the terrible things that happened to us. Those memories don't serve us. They are not necessary, and they impede further movement in your healing and growth. While we can agree that wrong has been done and deep loss has occurred, it does not help us to be reminded of these things. Feel the feelings when they show up, hand them over to Jesus, and refocus on the freedom.

The valley of rejection is rich with fertile soil. Depending on what we plant and nurture, the valley will either produce life-giving fruit, or a bitter, unhealthy crop of brokenness. What we feed will grow. So remembering and focusing on the miraculous goodness of God will develop in us a beautiful new sense of purpose.

> The valley of rejection is rich with fertile soil. Depending on what we plant and nurture, the valley will either produce life-giving fruit, or a bitter, unhealthy crop of brokenness.

KEY TAKEAWAYS

- Remember the Giver of the gifts.

- Keep track of what you have learned in the valley—this is your ministry.

- Remember what God has brought you out of, and what He is calling you toward.

- Freedom on the other side of the valley can lead to complacency in our Christian life.

REJECTION RECOVERY

Only be careful, and watch yourselves closely so that you do not forget the things your eyes have seen or let them slip from your heart as long as you live. Teach them to your children and to their children after them (Deuteronomy 4:9).

THERAPEUTIC QUESTIONS

- What gets in the way of remembering to remember all of the things God has done for you?
- If these obstacles to remembering are permitted to stay, what might happen to your ministry?
- What passages were significant to you during the deepest part of your valley and why?
- If you could create a reminder, a symbol or item to help you remember God's goodness and His Hands in your life, what would that be?

JOURNAL PROMPT

These are the things I want to hold in my heart as things God has taught me, shown me, healed me from.

Thank you, Lord, for all You have done for me and through me. I have learned so much about You during this time in the valley, and Your love for me leaves me speechless. I want to remember Your work, and what You have done so that I can minister to others who are in pain. I give you my story, please use it for Your glory. Amen.

PART 3

Reclaiming Your True Identity

CHAPTER 11

An Identity of Free

"She had not known the weight, until she felt the freedom."

—Hester, *The Scarlet Letter*

I'm not a runner. In fact, if you ever see me running, you should run too—something very troublesome is bearing down on all of us. When I have run in the past, it's visually unappealing and physically agonizing. All the things go in all the directions. I sweat profusely, and I can literally feel my lungs trying to kill me. Running is not even a little bit my thing, and I deeply admire you incredible women who do it.

Running was Claire's thing though. Remember Claire? The beautiful young woman who faced excruciating abuse and rejection by her parents? Claire was a long-distance runner, and it was when she was running that she felt the most free. When Claire arrived in her perfectly put together Lulu outfit, devastation and grief had stolen her interest in this beloved hobby.

Prior to the trauma of court and the rejection by her mom, Claire enjoyed numerous church activities, was training for her first marathon, and was pursuing ministry. Rejection left a trail of debris in its wake and along with many other things, Claire stopped running. Claire carried with her a long list of losses.

Rejection does this, doesn't it? There's a before and an after, marked by the pivot point of rejection. Life before we are rejected, and then life after. Our life before rejection had a rhythm with a system we knew how to navigate—not always easy, but familiar. And the life after feels like living in a Boggle® shaker where everything is mixed up and thrown out in tumbling pieces. In the tumbling, we lose things that are important to us.

The losses add up. For many, rejection takes away beloved hobbies and activities. While for others, relationships we hold dear and people we thought would be with us forever, join the list of casualties. We choose some losses when shame seeps in and convinces us we are unworthy of the things and people we love, prompting a letting go, or a walking away. We stop investing, because we believe the mental narrative declaring our lack of value. We drift away from the people and activities we love through a convincing internal declaration of unworthiness.

It's as though the trauma of rejection gets the final say about our worth in the lives of everyone around us. *I am not good enough for this relationship. We don't have anything in common anymore.* And, as with Claire's loss of running, it contaminates our joy-filled activities through the onset of depression and shame.

Some losses are imposed on us through the natural order of things. No question, loss is an aspect of rejection. Things change, and as we navigate the new, we experience the shift in activities and relationships.

- We used to golf together, and the rejection means I lost my golfing partner.
- Kayaking isn't as much fun without him.
- Travelling was our thing, but it's not easy or safe to travel as a single person.

- My in-laws stepped away, even though they were hurting and confused too.
- Friendships we established as a couple are rocky through the initial months of separation. And when the new normal finds its ground, we are left with a surprisingly small collection of loyalists.
- I no longer frequent that restaurant, attend that event, or belong to that club, because it hurts too much.

Claire lost many things in her life, and the rejection story was thick as she sat in my office. Somehow during the course of our work, running became her measuring stick for healing.

When she first arrived in my office, she told me she had lost interest in her favorite activity. Burdened by the broken heart of rejection, she sometimes looked at her running shoes with contempt. They seemed to taunt her from their home in the hall, and every day as she walked past them, the shame grew inside her. Sometimes she kicked the shoes in anger. And for a period of time, she demoted them to a semi-sheltered location outside her front door.

As she travelled her road to recovery, Claire noticed a shift in her feelings about her running shoes. She began to feel less anger and less shame. And as time moved, so did the shoes. One day, Claire sat down on the floor beside her beloved running shoes and pulled them up on her lap. She looked long and hard at these shoes, molded perfectly to her runner's feet.

Feeling the laces in her hand made her smile. She ran her fingers over the tread and noticed small stones stuck in the bottoms. Turning the shoes over, her eyes landed on a powerful message from her younger self. Scribbled and barely there, on the sole of her right shoe were the words, "Yes, you can." And on the left, "Don't quit. No matter what."

Pivot.

Claire sat in silence for a long time, staring at the words from the heart of her younger self.

Rejection had threatened to take running away from Claire. And more than that, it threatened to take Claire off the course God had called her to.

My friend, how dare it? How dare the bad behaviour of one person—the hurtful, harmful activities of another, infiltrate our lives in this way? Rejection and its team of co-accusers does not get to steal any more from us!

Through many months of counseling and countless face-to-knee moments together, Claire began to accept a different story about herself. She decided to reject the rejection story and rebel against the lies circulating in her heart as a result of the carelessness of others. She was not rejectable. And when the day came for Claire to lace up her shoes and take her first run of freedom, she laughed and cried her way through the familiar streets in her neighbourhood.

Almost ten years have passed since Claire sat in my office, but her story has touched my heart deeply. The beautiful, broken-hearted young woman I met all those years ago is now a licensed trauma informed counselor herself. She is a leader in her church and enjoys a full life with her pastor husband and their children. And she just completed her fourth marathon.

How? How did the healing happen for Claire? How did she cling to hope when the rejection story gripped her deeply? When the abandonment from childhood haunted her, spewing lies about her worth and value?

She considered and eventually accepted an alternate story.

Claire had believed since childhood there was something wrong with her, something shameful that limited her worth and made her disposable. This childhood wound collected momentum as life experiences and ongoing letdowns fueled the fire and reinforced the rejection message. When Claire considered a different perspective and challenged the human-imposed message with a divine message of truth, she began to see herself through a different lens.

Divine messages of truth must inform the new narrative if we are going to move out of the valley of rejection and into the life God has for us. Moving away from a rejection-informed lens and toward a God-informed lens gives us a new perspective and sets our feet back in motion. This new stride based on our changed perspective allows us to hover above the rejection story and collect meaning from the things that have happened to us.

> Moving away from a rejection-informed lens and toward a God-informed lens gives us a new perspective and sets our feet back in motion.

Journey to Healing

> Meaning making is an essential component of healing from rejection.

Meaning making is an essential component of healing from rejection. We must move from hurting to hoping to helping. During my intensive research in the valley of rejection, I scoured the Bible for women like me—broken, rejected, replaced—and I begged God to show me how He used these women.

Meet my favorite woman of the Bible, the Samaritan at the well. It was just like any other day for this beautiful, yet broken soul, as she made her way to fetch her water. The blistering sun was high in the sky. I picture her wrapped in a stola to protect her from the fiery heat.

The journey to this well was about half a mile, and in the heat of the day, it would have been a painfully long walk. Perhaps more painful than the heat was the vicious voice in her head that recited shame-inspired messages on repeat. And maybe more painful again, the words spewed at her over the years as she navigated the rollercoaster of rejection, trauma, betrayal, abuse, and grief. Harmful words. Hateful words. Words from the men she called husbands, words from people who had once been her friends, childhood playmates, and family.

She wore her shame like a second garment, and with each dusty step, she carried her water jar and her trauma farther from the city. I imagine her on this day, watching her dust-covered feet cover the same road she had walked for years, choosing the well on the outskirts of town. My heart longs to comfort her. I would say, "Me too, I see you Sister. I would have walked to this distant well too. I get the shame that makes you feel small and unworthy. I understand the grief that calls you to isolate and stay unseen. Walk the greater distance, to feel the lesser pain. That makes sense to me."

But today was different for our sweet friend as she plodded along. Can you imagine looking into the distance and seeing a man sitting at the well? A Jewish man, no less, and in her culture someone superior. Knowing the kind of pain she held, I wonder if she wrestled with how to behave in that moment.

Was she afraid? Did she wonder if He wanted something from her? Many men had made assumptions about her based on the story she carried. What thoughts ran through her mind? Men had not been kind to our Samaritan friend, and her soul wounds would have been deep as she wondered about this man. Wondered about His intentions.

I like to believe the moment they made eye contact her soul knew Him. I can only imagine the stirring in her spirit as she wondered about the magnetic pull this man had, as though He already knew her, and He could see into her heart.

In John 4, the Bible tells us that Jesus was travelling to Galilee from Judea to continue His ministry. Jews typically travelled the long way around Samaria. But not Jesus. Sending His disciples into town for food, He sat at the well alone, waiting for our friend. What would Jesus have been thinking and feeling as He watched her approach?

He knew her story. He knew she had been married five times, and that she was living with a man who was not her husband. But more than that, He knew her pain. He saw her heart.

As with so many recorded conversations with Jesus, this interaction begins with a question to a broken heart and ends with a passionate declaration of His transforming love. The Bible doesn't tell us how long they visited, but we know the pivot point was Jesus.

Our friend arrives at the well with a thick rejection narrative in her heart but, after one interaction with Jesus, she embraces a new identity and a new story. Her heart renewed and her hope restored, our sister runs back to town, leaving her water jug at the well.

She runs.

I love the image of our sister running. Tears of joy flowing down her dusty, sun worn cheeks, one hand frantically waving to anyone who could see her. The other hand holding her dress, making way for the legs that had once carried her shame-filled frame away from town.

Her feet now carried a new story, and her soul had been profoundly touched by her time with Jesus.

"Come and see a man who told me everything I ever did. Could he possibly be the Messiah?" (John 4:29), she declares with excitement.

The Bible tells us many became believers because of her testimony. Our broken, shame-filled Samaritan sister became a messenger for Jesus.

Formerly a moral outcast, now set free and running back to town to make way for the Saviour. Rejected right into the arms of the Greatest Love she had ever known. Once overwhelmed with loss, now set free and restored because of one visit with her Messiah.

Riding Shotgun

Freedom is waiting for us. As with our ancient sister, the past does not get the final say in who we are. The things done and said to us hold no weight when we carry them to the feet of Jesus and ask Him to hold them.

Maybe, like me, you wince at the past, wishing away choices you've made. And perhaps, like me, you struggle to leave the shame-based messages behind you. There are things holding us back from being the person God wants us to be.

Freedom is a choice. We either accept it, or we don't. But when we do, when we decide to own this new identity and declare ourselves free, we get to ride shotgun for the unfolding of God's plan for our lives.

When we hold up our deepest wounds and greatest losses to Jesus, offering them to Him with an expectant heart, He will absolutely bring beauty from the brokenness. This is what Jesus does, isn't it? He reframes the rejection story, picks up the shattered pieces, and reminds us who we are to Him. And then He makes us messengers of His profound love and unbelievable grace.

KEY TAKEAWAYS

- Rejection creates a pivot point—a before and after that changes everything.

- God calls us to live free: free of shame, free of anxiety, and free of the labels slapped onto us by others or ourselves.

- While rejection feels oppressive, we are called into freedom.

- Our brokenness can be healed when we turn it over to Jesus.

- There is ministry in the mess and purpose in the pain.

REJECTION RECOVERY

"For I know the plans I have for you', says the LORD. 'They are plans for good and not for disaster, to give you a future and a hope" (Jeremiah 29:11 NLT).

THERAPEUTIC QUESTIONS

- What is rejection learning about you through this season that it might be concerned about?

- If rejection knew God was going to use your story to bless others, what would it say?

- Consider the Samaritan woman at the well. What part of her conversation with Jesus do you think would have been most liberating for her?

- If you were waiting in Samaria when the woman returned from her talk with Jesus, what would she tell you to help you with your own healing?

JOURNAL PROMPT

What would you say to the Samaritan woman if you were walking with her that day to the well?

Jesus, I don't know how to thank you for waiting for me at the well. I don't want to be so connected to my pain story that I miss the opportunity to be fully healed by You. I want to be a messenger for You, and I want You to use my pain to help others. Please help me to be a good steward of my story. I give You permission to move me in the direction You want me to go. Thank you for loving me so much that you will seek me out, cross borders, and pursue me. Amen.

CHAPTER 12

An Identity of Overcomer

"Out of suffering have emerged the strongest souls; the most massive characters are seared with scars."

—Khalil Gibran

Weak moments do not make you a weak person. More than that, weak moments do not define your level of trust in God or your faith. The destabilizing impact of rejection has a ripple effect, and it has thrown us off kilter. Okay, it's kicked our blessed behinds. But it has not wrecked us, and we are not powerless.

Working with women for most of my career has afforded me the wonderful gift of meeting victorious overcomers. Some of them have faced brokenness we only read about in fiction books, reminding me that having good bounce back is not a fictional, hoped-for response to pain and tragedy. These women have been face down on the valley floor. They felt weak, but they stood up anyway. And in their choice to move forward, they remembered Who was in control.

> Weak moments do not make you a weak person.

She Calls Me Mom

I am particularly inspired by the young woman who calls me Mom. When I think about victorious overcoming—she comes to mind.

Take for example, the day she flew off the stage at her high school graduation.

Over one thousand people filled the auditorium. And as my oh-so-clumsy, perfectly unique, wonderfully-made seventeen-year-old shuffled her way to the front of the stage, I held my breath.

High school had been rough for her. Managing anxiety and depression had become a full-time job. And after a particularly difficult season of pain, she decided a new school would help with the struggle. Exhibiting incredible courage, she left her small rural school in the middle of her senior year and transferred to the largest public school in the city.

And there she stood on her graduation day. Beaming with pride, amongst a sea of faces she didn't know. My heart was full as I watched her. We had bought an elegant new dress for the event, and her perfectly-styled hair showcased the beautiful face of the girl I loved so much.

She had been through a lot, this girl of mine. Wrestling with a sense of abandonment, spurred by abuse from peers and the daily struggle of trying to fit in, left her battling for a safe place to land. But on this day, all the loss and pain seemed to drift off into the background. And adjusting her grad hat with authority, she took a fateful step toward the edge of the stage.

It's a bit of a blur in my mind, what happened next. Suddenly, with absolutely no grace or finesse, my daughter stumbled, teetered, and then literally launched off the stage in the most dramatic wipe-out I had ever seen. She body surfed down the steps, ripping her gown, breaking her cap, and landed with a thud on the floor.

Gasps, and then an audible hush flooded the auditorium. People clamoured to her rescue, and all eyes were fixed on the pretzel-shaped teenager at the bottom of the stairs.

But this girl is amazing. And no public humiliation was going to hold her back. In a masterful moment of resilience, she popped off the floor, steadied herself on her fancy shoes, and with arms raised high into the air and a victorious smile on her face, she yelled, "I'm okay!"

And just like that, with her bold declaration, the entire auditorium erupted with enthusiastic cheers of celebration. High fives awaited her as she hobbled her way to her seat. And laughter rang through the audience as people regrouped with relief that this young lady was okay.

Without a doubt, this memorable display of resilience earned her a reputation among her peers, and she continues to be known as "That girl who fell off the stage at grad."

But do you know what I remember?

I remember the girl who fell off the stage *and then got back up*. I remember the silence at her fall and the celebration at her recovery. I remember the high fives, hugs, and relieved faces welcoming her as she limped her way through the masses.

And I remember the beautiful, smiling face greeting me after the ceremony. The torn gown, broken cap, and rug-burned knees told the story of a girl who took quite a tumble. But her face held the expression of a young woman who experienced an incredible victory. The unthinkable had happened, and there she stood, smiling. It's not the fall that stands out for me, it's the recovery. And you know what, I was unbelievably proud of my overcomer.

It's How We Roll

Reflecting back on my daughter's graduation mishap, I see myself in her story. And maybe you can relate too. Life is full of wipeouts and broken cap situations. We trip and tumble through difficulties that threaten to take us totally off course. Sometimes we bounce up, dust ourselves off, adjust the cap, declare, "I'm okay," and move forward. While other times, we stay face down on the floor for a time, not sure how to get up, or how to be okay.

> Overcomers don't stay face down for long, the only place to grow resilience is in the struggle.

But overcomers don't stay face down for long, the only place to grow resilience is in the struggle. We can't be victims and victors at the same time. Very bad things happen to us, and as Christians we are not guaranteed freedom from pain. In fact, the opposite is true. In John 16:33b, Jesus says, *"In the world you will have trouble. But take heart! I have overcome the world."* While there is some bad news in this Scripture, the overcomer in me sees the hope. "Take heart! I have overcome the world!" What beautiful words spoken by Jesus, the Ultimate Overcomer.

Overcoming is not a new phenomenon—people have been doing it throughout the history of the world. Eve was the first overcomer. Her grave mistake in the garden not only altered the course of history, it also hurt God deeply. Her sin brought tremendous shame. The resulting eviction from Eden meant brokenness and pain would be Eve's companions for the rest of her life. I hold no judgement toward Eve. Knowing myself, I am certain I would have done the same thing.

We know how Eve's life went—her oldest son killed her youngest son. And just like that, Eve became the mother of a murdered boy, while simultaneously becoming the mother of a murderer. It takes my breath away when I think of it. The loss she faced, and the guilt she felt, both must have been paralyzing.

Beautiful Eve, your heartbreak must have felt unbearable.

A victorious overcomer, Eve did not let her mistakes keep her from returning into a right relationship with God. While some think of her as a faulty ancestor whose choices meant hardship for the rest of us, I think of her as a remarkable trailblazer, a reminder that God does not give up on us. She later gave birth to Seth, a child she raised to love and honour God.

> Our mistakes do not have to take us away from our Heavenly Father.

Our mistakes do not have to take us away from our Heavenly Father. While sin and the resulting shame seek to separate us from Him, Our Heavenly Father isn't going anywhere. In the garden, God sought out His children after they sinned. And even today, in our own lives—He is still pursuing us.

Fast forward with me to a day in the life of a desperate woman who had a life-changing moment with Jesus. She had been bleeding for twelve years. Can we just take a moment to grieve for her. Twelve years, ladies. Twelve! Some versions of the Bible suggest she was hemorrhaging . . . for twelve years. I'm speechless just thinking about how this must have impacted her life.

We meet her on a day in Capernaum, as she breaks cultural norms and grabs hold of Jesus' robe. The Bible tells us this woman had suffered a great deal under the care of many doctors who had treated her badly and taken her for all of her resources. After considerable, unsuccessful treatments, her health only worsened. The physical discomfort and weakness would have been unbearable, but it's the resulting emotional devastation that stands out to me.

Considered unclean, our friend would have faced excruciating rejection and loneliness. Anything she touched was considered unclean. Anyone who touched what she touched, would have been considered unclean.

Women in her community lived their lives, had children and enjoyed friendship, but she was not part of that. Her illness left her an outsider. How long had it been since someone who loved her hugged or held her? When was the last time she felt seen for who she was?

Physically and emotionally debilitated, she continued to drag herself to doctors, desperate for healing, but finding none.

What did it feel like that day—to hear about Jesus? Did she let herself hope?

I picture her wasted body as she covers herself and makes her way to where He is. The crowd is thick, and Jesus is not just surrounded. The Bible tells us, *"A great crowd followed him and thronged about Him"* (Mark 5: 24b ESV). It was more of a mob scene than a stroll for Jesus, and our friend is determined to reach Him—unstoppable and intent. This woman is tenacious.

Intuitively, she knew what she needed to do. *"If I just touch His clothes, I will be healed"* (Mark 5:28b), she told herself. Reaching through the crowd, she felt her fingers make contact, and immediately the bleeding stopped. Her health was restored.

Imagine what this would have been like for her. Healed on the spot. Knowing someone had touched Him, Jesus turned to see her.

He knew who He was looking for, He always does. Falling at His feet, she explains to Him what happened. His voice is gentle, as

He speaks directly to her. *"Daughter, your faith has healed you. Go in peace and be freed from your suffering"* (Mark 5:34).

In an instant, Jesus healed our sick sister. Her faith-informed decision drove her to move toward Jesus, reach out to Him, and believe He would fix what was broken. It required a decision to do the hard thing, to put her faith in the One she knew would save her. The key ingredient in a new identity of victorious overcoming is Jesus. Without Him, the bounce back is rooted in human limitations.

> The key ingredient in a new identity of victorious overcoming is Jesus. Without Him, the bounce back is rooted in human limitations.

Hope-Inspired Determination

Jesus was the ultimate Overcomer. His life is marked by a series of rejections and losses. He faced ridicule, rejection, disloyalty, and disappointment we will never fully understand. For the three years of His ministry, our Saviour lived and loved with divine purity. Even then, He was scoffed at, rumours were spread, and even His closest friends turned their backs.

In His perfection, He was rejected. Even though He loved fiercely, He was misunderstood, abused, and forsaken. In my darker days in the valley, it brought me considerable comfort to realize how much Jesus understood my pain. He understood abandonment. Promises were made to Him and then broken. Loyal friends and loved ones turned their backs on Him. The rejection He faced as a man continues even to this day, as the ones He loves walk away.

But overcoming is our Saviour's specialty. In His life and His death, Jesus models for us the focus on the Father. He did not let the words of the many influence the truth about Him. In an incredible display of victory, Jesus was murdered, buried, and then rose from the dead, reminding us that He understands suffering and if we let Him, leads the way to victory.

> Overcomers are built in the difficulties of life.

Overcomers are built in the difficulties of life. Rooted in the belief that God will make good on His promises, we walk with hope-inspired determination in the direction of His call on our lives. Our ministry will be most effective when we can share the victory story of how God brought us through and gave us a new identity of Overcomer.

KEY TAKEAWAYS

- Overcoming is an act of will and is not reliant on feelings or circumstances.

- Weak moments do not make us weak people.

- Weak moments do not mean we have weak faith.

- Our mistakes do not define us, nor do the mistakes of others.

- Victorious overcomers are built in the difficulties of life.

REJECTION RECOVERY

Consider it pure joy, my brothers and sisters, whenever you face trials of many kinds, because you know that the testing of your faith produces perseverance (James 1:2-3).

THERAPEUTIC QUESTIONS

- If Overcoming were up against Rejection and its Co-Accusers, how would that conversation go?

- If you were to fully embrace the God-given identity of Overcomer, what would change in your life?

- Reflect back on your younger self, the woman at the start of this journey. Do you see how you have embraced a victory mentality?

- What stands in the way of fully embracing this new identity?

JOURNAL PROMPT

What would your older self say to you today, the person standing fully in an identity of victorious overcomer?

Jesus, you are the ultimate Overcomer. Thank you for your example of victory in pain. And thank you for this new identity. Please help me to keep my eyes on the victory You offer—to stay focused on overcoming, and moving toward You, even when it's hard. I trust You and I believe in You, Lord. Amen.

CHAPTER 13

An Identity of Courage

"A ship is always safe at shore, but that is not what it's built for."

—ALBERT EINSTEIN

It was 1964, and Joy was pregnant. It was uncommon to have a baby at the young age of sixteen, but Joy decided to complete her pregnancy and place her baby up for adoption. With the announcement of her pregnancy came a landslide of changes, and a litany of shame induced messages about her worth.

No longer able to attend high school, she was enrolled in a business program and moved to a new city, into the home of her older brother where she prepared for the birth of her baby. And three months before her seventeenth birthday, Joy gave birth to her son.

Hospital policy required newborns be removed from their birthmothers immediately following delivery and placed with interim families to await placement in their adoptive homes. But the nurse on duty mistakenly brought the baby to Joy. And for two precious hours, she held her son before the staff took him away.

She left the hospital without her child. For many months her body went through all the postpartum changes, reminding her daily she was a mom, but her arms were empty—acting as reminders of her loss. She grieved her son alone and held her secret pain as she continued with her life. But out there somewhere was a boy she loved and thought of every day.

For almost forty years, Joy wondered about her son. And in 2002, with emotions I will never fully understand, the opportunity came to meet him.

I have an intimate knowing of her courage, because this amazing woman is my mom. Since their reunion almost twenty years ago, my mom has used her testimony and her experience with heartache to speak to women who have questioned God's goodness and grace.

In every way her courage has inspired others and left a ripple effect of hope in the lives of the people around her.

Thank You for Your Courage

Hardship invites a choice—to move forward or shrink back. We get to decide. The absence of pain and struggle sounds delightful, but it certainly doesn't grow or build us. It's both a good news story and a bad news story at the same time. We want courage, we like the idea of it, but without fear, without an obstacle, without pain, it really can't exist.

> I don't like being scared. But I do like being courageous.

I don't like being scared. But I do like being courageous. And this valley has us calling on our courage in a moment-by-moment battle of the wills. Through my field research in the valley, I needed reminders that I was not alone. So, pen in hand, I embraced the mission of finding the most courageous historical characters in the Bible. And then, because they deserve it, I wrote them thank you notes.

> *Dear Moses,*
> *Thank you for having the courage to face the past and lead the people through terrifying situations. You wrestled hard with identity. Even though you felt inadequate, unsure, and scared, you obeyed God. Your courage to do the work you were called to do reminds me to do the same.*

Dear Samaritan woman at the well,
Thank you for having the courage to face rejection and grief, the courage to accept healing from Jesus, and then return to your village boldly proclaiming the Good News. You inspire me to be brave and to not let the opinions of others limit my calling.

Dear King David,
Thank you for having the courage to face impossible problems and rely heavily on God for everything. Thank you for writing the Psalms, because I needed your words. Your courage to confess and repent, to admit your shortcomings and reclaim God's direction for your life, is a wonderful example of humility.

Dear Rahab,
Thank you for having the courage to step outside of your reputation and put your faith in God. Your courage to trust God to redeem your story has inspired me more than you know. Thank you for showing me that the past doesn't get to take me away from being useful to Jesus.

Dear Joseph,
Thank you for having the courage to forgive your brothers and to continue to love in spite of such a painful betrayal. And thank you for your example of owning your uniqueness and letting God use you. You remind me that the sins of others and the wrongs done to me don't interfere with God's plans.

Dear Queen Esther,
Thank you for having the courage to take risks and rise above the cultural obstacles, limiting expectations, and systems of oppression that sought to hold you back. Thank you for doing the right thing, even when the outcome felt uncertain.

Dear Daniel,
Thank you for having the courage to not give in when the odds were against you and to trust God even when things looked bleak. Thank you for trusting God so much that you were full of hope even when others wanted you harmed. Your determined faith and boldness inspire me to claim the Truth in spite of circumstances.

Dear Woman Who Bled,
Thank you for having the courage to seek healing and pursue Jesus even through pain and suffering. Your courage to hope, trust, and believe reminds me to always reach out to Jesus.

Dear Mary,
Thank you for having the courage to accept the mission God gave you and for honouring Him with your life. Thank you for raising Jesus, a perfect child, and for managing all that entailed.

Dear Job,
Thank you for having the courage to face gut wrenching heartache and countless losses, while maintaining your trust in the goodness of God and His purpose of your life.

Dear Jesus,
Thank you for having the courage to stand up and turn the other cheek—and to face injustice, betrayal, rejection, and death. Even death on a cross. I can't imagine the courage it must have taken to accept the mission and stay the course, even when everything was crumbling, and Your closest people fled. Thank you for not giving up on us, and for Your unshakeable love that drove You to pursue us at such a cost. Your sacrifice shows me how much you love me, and how much you want me.

Courage as Your Coat of Armour

Towering in our not-too-distant past is the formidable, pain-inducing obstacle of rejection. It sought to break you, much like Joseph's brothers sought to break him. It wanted to make you small, infusing messages of inadequacy, like the woman at the well. And it wanted to steal you away from God's plan, taunting you with lies and infiltrating your life with messages not meant for you, just like Rahab and Moses.

And here you are, on the other side of rejection, capturing a new vision and owning a new identity of courage. Like our ancestors, we cannot be courageous without the presence of fear, pain, or uncertainty. They modelled courage for us. And their stories have travelled through the centuries to remind us that suffering and sorrow are not new problems. Standing up under the weight of pain is not impossible. As I've reflected on their lives and sat in awe of the brave and courageous people in the Bible, I've found myself wondering if they would use the word courage to describe themselves. Did they consider themselves brave?

Courage can be hard to see in ourselves. From our perspective, we can clearly see all the areas our elders stood up to, in the face of fear. They wore courage like armour through the valleys in their lives, and they left a legacy of tenacious heroism and bravery for us following in their footsteps. Their testimony continues to reach through the pages of history and remind people like you and me that courage is not the absence of wobbly knees, sweaty palms, and tears.

Courage is the determination to not be undone by circumstances—regardless of how painful it may be. It's feeling the fear and moving forward anyways. Courage holds determination by the hand, tips its hat to uncertainty, and pushes through.

> Courage holds determination by the hand, tips its hat to uncertainty, and pushes through.

Do you know what I love most about courage? Once we get it, once we face the obstacles and push through the fears, no one can

An Identity of Courage

take that away. We will always have it. The more challenges we face, the more courage we build. And very soon, after all the pain is gone and the obstacles dot the past, we still get to own this truth—courage belongs to the overcomer.

Your suffering is not pointless. In fact, if I can guess, the heartache of rejection and the loss you've faced will serve to inform great things in your life.

How do I know this? Because the courage it has taken to get this far through the valley is a testament to your perseverance and determination to heal. And God loves to use the testimony of overcomers. He will not waste your pain.

Your story is not a surprise to God. He isn't scratching His head, wondering what happened or how this is going to end. He hasn't changed His mind about you because of what has happened or what you have or haven't done. Our Heavenly Father is an active, attentive, invested Parent who has remained present for every twist and turn in your valley.

Courage is defined as "mental or moral strength to venture, persevere, and withstand danger or difficulty."[5] Brene Brown says, "Courage is the ability to show up and be seen when you can't control the outcome."[6]

Biblical courage relies on the supernatural power of God to strengthen and motivate the believer. Romans 5:3–5 reminds us, *"Not only that, but we rejoice in our sufferings, knowing that suffering produces endurance, and endurance produces character, and character produces hope, and hope does not put us to shame, because God's love has been poured into our hearts through the Holy Spirit who has been given to us"* (ESV). Embracing the struggle as an opportunity for growth and knowing we are not doing this alone, will empower us to stay the course.

Faces of Courage

We are among the courageous. We have felt the sting of betrayal and rejection, or the loss of love, and the unwanted changes chosen for us. But we refuse to be undone by the awful. Like our biblical ancestors we have a story of faith-infused overcoming, and we are the present day faces of courage.

Diane is one of the most courageous women I have ever known. Having lost three of her four children to a terrible disease, Diane remains steadfast in her love and commitment to God. She declares Him trustworthy and loving—believing He knows best, even though her heart has been broken in ways most of us can never fathom. My beautiful friend clings to hope, knowing she will be reunited with her children one day.

Thank you, Diane, for the courage to hold on to faith through heartache and inspire others to do the same.

Joanne's dad left their family when she was fourteen. Her mom went into a serious depression and took too many pills. Joanne called 911, and then stepped into her mothers shoes, caring for her siblings while her mom battled mental illness for years. Later in her life, Joanne developed a program for children of parents with mental health concerns. She has made it her mission to help young people lean on Jesus for comfort—the only True source of strength.

Thank you, Joanne, for having the courage to step into shoes and a role that frightened you. Your courage is a love letter to your family and an inspiration to those who know your story.

Renee lost two husbands to alcoholism. They didn't die, they left. But their leaving was not without months of horror and trauma that still haunt her at times even now. She found shelter for herself and her children, she stood in line at the foodbank as needed, and she worked toward her degree. Renee volunteered at her church, attended counseling, and over time, experienced healing from the damages done through the abuse in her life. Today, she runs groups for women who are living in the aftermath of addiction.

Thank you, Renee, for having the courage to recover from terrible things and to use your pain for a greater purpose.

How does your story read, friend? What courageous tale is true for you? The rejection recovery story you have lived is not purposeless. There is a divine vision for our lives, and while God has a carefully orchestrated plan, He is not going to force it on us. It takes courage to get this far, and it will continue to take courage to move even further through this valley and into the vision.

Our role in the vision has three courageous parts.

1. The courage to *accept the vision* God has for us, letting go of the former identity holding us back.

2. The courage to *let go of the controls.* Let go of the pain and release it to Jesus.

3. The courage to *trust Him to lead us through* and the belief that He will.

It's time to accept your new identity, and move forward with God's vision for you.

Like you, I'm learning to embrace this new identity. I love to savour the sweetness of recovery, and within that is this newfound desire to build my identity of courage. Put on this new coat, my friend. I think you will find it fits exactly right.

KEY TAKEAWAYS

- Courage is not the absence of fear—but rather the determination to feel the fear and move forward in spite of it.

- Biblical courage requires us to use the supernatural to face our fears.

- There is a divine vision for your life—courage is necessary to move forward in it.

- Your story of courage is being written even now as you work through this valley.

REJECTION RECOVERY

Be strong and courageous. Do not be afraid or terrified because of them, for the LORD your God goes with you; He will never leave you nor forsake you (Deuteronomy 31:6).

THERAPEUTIC QUESTIONS

- What does courage mean to you? How do you know you're living a life of courage?

- What does courage bring to the table that rejection might struggle with?

- If being bold and courageous was a movie, what would it be about?

- Considering what you know about rejection, do you think courage is a worthy adversary? Why or why not?

JOURNAL PROMPT

Your new identity of courage means you face hard things. What does that look like going forward?

Jesus, you are the best example of courage and boldness. I admit there are many times I feel less than, scared, and uncertain. But you have not called me to have a spirit of timidity. Rather You want me to stand up under the pain and face my new life with a posture of strength and courage. I don't always feel bold, and I certainly don't always feel courageous. Please help me be the woman of courage you want me to be. I trust you Lord to fill me with what I need to stand for you, to show others what you have done through me. Amen.

CHAPTER 14

An Identity of Wanted & Chosen

"And this is the marvel of marvels; that He called me beloved."

—C.S. LEWIS

Counselors need counseling too. And on that particular day, I was in deep need of an appointment. I hadn't been sleeping well. Coming to terms with my new identity was taking a toll, and my emotions were locked and loaded. It had been almost a year since he left and in so many ways, things were going well. So, the sudden onslaught of grief blindsided me, and of course, infused me with doubt about my healing.

Sinking into Jenny's counseling couch, I crossed my legs and looked at her with what I'm sure was a face of pain, mixed with hope and peppered with exhaustion. She met my eyes with compassion, and like every good counselor would, she asked, "What's happening for you today?"

Jenny was no stranger to this pain. She herself had walked through a similar valley. As she held space for me in that room, I felt her understanding. She listened as I shared my heart with her and after several minutes, with gentleness and wisdom, she said, "Nicole, do you think God is wrong about you?"

I didn't know what to say, but my pride rose to the occasion. With flatness that surprised me, I answered, "Maybe."

Let's be honest here, rejection is an agonizing assault on self-esteem. Healing from the blow of marital abandonment is a courageous and intentional climb out of the mess and into a new identity.

It does not leave anyone feeling favoured. And it does not feel like a blessing. But blessings don't always get wrapped up in pretty packages, do they? Jenny earned her hourly rate that day, as she gently and deliberately walked me through the reminders God had left for me in His Word:

> Blessings don't always get wrapped up in pretty packages.

- He created me in His image and breathed life into me (Genesis 1:27, Genesis 2:7).
- The hairs of my head are known (Matthew 10:30).
- I am fearfully and wonderfully made (Psalm 139:14).
- I am knitted together and intricately woven (Psalm 139: 13, 15).
- I am chosen, holy, and beloved (Colossians 3:12).
- I am crowned with glory and honour (Psalm 8:5).
- He gave His only Son for me (John 3:16).
- The old has passed away, the new has come (2 Corinthians 5:17).
- I am forgiven and no longer condemned (1 John 1:9, Roman. 8:1–2).
- I am justified, redeemed, and cleansed (Romans 5:1, 1 John 1:7, 9).
- I am completely safe and secure in God's love. Nothing can separate us (Romans 8:39, John 10:29).
- I am victorious in Jesus (1 Corinthians 15:17).
- I have a glorious future (Romans 8:18).
- I am deeply loved and the King of kings gave His life in pursuit of me (John 3:16).

A New Name

There was a period of thick silence as I leafed eagerly through my Bible, highlighting and underlining these beautiful passages. Counselors are trained in silence. We don't get squirmy or feel awkward in it, because we understand the therapeutic benefit of just sitting still in the moment. As we sat in her office, Bibles open on our laps, the heaviness in my heart began to lift. I began to write:

> Chosen - not rejected.
> Favoured - not disposable.
> Beloved - not neglectable.
> Known - not forgettable.
> Pursued - not forgotten.
> Seen - not invisible.
> Wanted - not replaceable.

Jenny wasn't done. She had kept impressive notes on the many signs and wonders I had shared with her during our several months of work together.

God had not been silent in my life. He had shown up in some of the tiniest details and also in the most powerful and meaningful ways. Jenny began to recite the list of reminders from my everyday life that had served as beacons of hope from God Himself. There were countless beautiful people who loved me well, an apartment that fit me perfectly, generous movers who discounted my moving rate, and an undeniable sense of purpose in my heart. The fingerprints of Jesus were everywhere in my life. It's as though He very personally created a customized recovery plan for me, reminding me at every turn that He was with me.

Why do we forget to remember? Why do we struggle to notice His kindness all around us? What we nurture will grow, and I had been nurturing the loss.

I was caught up in what wasn't, rather than what was. I was focused on the loss and the wounds, rather than the healing and the gains. While I had indeed been rejected, and my family had faced a painful loss, I had also gained a new identity, and a new chance to live in line with who God had always called me to be.

As weird as this may sound, the rejection turned on the lights for me. I was learning to really see God. I was learning to recognize Him. And as I followed this learning into a closer intimacy with Jesus, I was understanding His love for me.

My brother and sister-in-law are talented musicians. They have faced their own valleys as a family, and through their pain they've written powerful music that continues to touch the lives of many people. A soothing balm on my broken heart, *Daughter of the Daylight* is one of my favorites from my sister-in-law. The lyrics of the first part of her song go like this:

> *I'm not a prisoner anymore.*
> *I am a daughter of Your Daylight,*
> *And when the night sends out its spies,*
> *descending subterfuge like flies,*
> *I'm not going to hear their lies,*
> *'cuz You are my destiny.*
> *Here in this respite of belief—I'm winged.*
> *Going to sleep in the comfort of pardon.*
> *Going to wake to the grace that's dawned.*
> *Going to dress in the colours of sunrise.*
> *Going to sing Your song.*
> *Every morning when Mercy wakes me.*

> *He says my name like a favored child.*
> *Going to sing, going to dance like the daughter of the Daylight.*
> *I wear the emblem of Your love,*
> *In jewels of hope and peace and trust.*
> *And they fit just like a glove,*
> *No more hand-me-downs of shame . . no no no,*
> *'cuz I hear Redemption call me by name.*[7]

> He says my name like a favoured child.

What words stand out for you in these beautiful lyrics? My eyes and heart land on, *He says my name like a favoured child.* In fact, the first time I really heard these words I was face down on my living room floor in my new prayer style. Starfished out in an ugly cry, desperate for a reminder that Jesus loves me, clinging to anything from His heart. I heard her angelic voice sing directly to my broken heart: *Nicole, He says your name like a favored child.*

He says our name like a favoured child!

Favoured. Child.

Let that soothe your soul today.

A Love Story to Root My Life On

> The underlying message throughout all of Scripture is a love story manifesting as God's grand pursuit, rooted in raw emotion, and a divine drive for connection with the children He created.

The theme of the Bible is Redemption. And the underlying message throughout all of Scripture is a love story manifesting as God's grand pursuit, rooted in raw emotion, and a divine drive for connection with the children He created. I have this image in my head of that pivotal conversation in Heaven. The one where Jesus agrees to accept the mission and leaves His home with His Father to live amongst us. How did that conversation go? Was Jesus reluctant to take on this task, knowing how it would end, realizing the emotional and physical anguish He would endure?

Absolutely not. He jumped at the idea. And with a heart full of love and an eagerness to make a way for His children, this divine strategy was rolled out in the most remarkable way. Jesus, in a profound act of love, left Heaven, pursuing His kids, and gave up His life to bring us Home. His chosen and favoured kids.

Why would He do this? What motivated Him?

The Bible tells us He was motivated by love. John 3:16 says, *"For God so loved the world that He gave His one and only Son, that whoever believes in Him should not perish but have eternal life."* These famous words from Jesus can get lost in their familiarity—but when we let ourselves really listen to the heart of our Heavenly Father, we feel His passion for us.

Favoured as an identity means we were chosen and hand-picked. Ephesians 1:4 says, *". . . even as He chose us in Him before the foundation of the world, that we should be holy and blameless before Him"* (ESV).

Before God brought about creation, He was thinking about you. And while He was making the mountains and telling the oceans where to stop, you and I were on His mind. He hung a star and thought of you. He built the landscape, thought up some wildlife, and smiled at the thought of you and all you bring to the world. He had you on His mind while He created the world, on His heart as He hung on the cross, and today as you continue to navigate this valley He wants you to remember what He says about you. Let His words be the truth in your identity.

His love drives Him to action because He doesn't want to be without you. You are favoured. And the circumstances that have you wondering about your worth and battling with your purpose do not change His feelings for you.

A Divine Reshuffling in Identity

When my daughter was about five years old, she had a close encounter with some earwigs, an insect indigenous to our area. While on a nature walk in the forest, she found a pet log to bring home. It was the mossiest, gnarliest log in the forest, and she wanted to make it her pet.

Determined to free it from the forest floor, she wrestled hard with this stump of wood for some time, dropping down to her knees, pushing with every last five-year-old pound. Finally, the log gave way with a surprising burst, landing her with an "umph" into the small, wet crater left in its path.

The earwigs rushed in all directions. Some made the fateful error of attaching themselves to my hysterical five-year-old, while others made way for cover, deep in the earth, away from the light.

When light is shed on darkness there's a frantic reshuffling that takes place. The Bible reminds us that our enemy is an opportunist (John 4:13), a liar (John 8:44), and a thief (John 10:10). He does not like it when we expose him to the light, and he gets squirmy when we declare our true identity—chosen children of the King.

When we accept a divine identity of chosen by Jesus, three things happen.

1. We measure everything said to us and about us against that Truth. This measuring stick allows us to reject the lies and the messages of the co-accusers. It insulates us against

rejections and letdowns, because being divinely chosen trumps all human opinion.

2. We move more intentionally in our lives with a sense of purpose and humble confidence. This new posture creates boundaries of influence in our lives. A boundary of influence means we are determined to live a certain way and refuse to settle for things less than what we are called to. We know Who holds us, we understand how significant we are to Him, and we realize we have a purpose. This knowing helps us move through our lives in a way that speaks to a closeness with Jesus.

3. We love others well and lead them toward an understanding of their own new identity in Jesus. A deep understanding of this new identity is hard to contain. The deficit story spinning in our hearts is replaced by a contagious enthusiastic knowing of the Truth. Being chosen and favoured is exciting, and when we feel that excitement, we want others to experience it too.

Living as a chosen child of The King is the ultimate identity. In fact, I can't think of anything I'd rather be. There are no human identities that compare. Being someone's spouse is special, but being wanted, chosen, and favoured by the King of Kings—that's next level special.

KEY TAKEAWAYS

- God is not wrong about you.

- Blessings aren't always wrapped in pretty packages.

- Jesus says your name like a favoured child.

- Favoured means you are chosen and handpicked.

- You have always been on God's mind.

- The enemy is desperate to sabotage your identity reconstruction.

- God's faithful favour gives us a safe place to land, to be seen, to be known and to be accepted.

REJECTION RECOVERY

For we are His workmanship, created in Christ Jesus for good works, which God prepared beforehand, that we should walk in them (Ephesians 2:10 ESV).

THERAPEUTIC QUESTIONS

- If you could interview your one-year-older self, the woman who has accepted her divine identity, what would she tell you about life in her shoes?

- What obstacles, mental narratives, or emotions might come in the way of accepting your identity of wanted, chosen, and favoured?

- When these show up, what can you call on to address these obstacles?

- How will you know when you have fully embraced your new identity of a chosen and favoured child of the King?

JOURNAL PROMPT

God is up to something in your life. He has chosen you for a purpose, and He calls you favoured. Let yourself be silent for a few moments and listen to God. What is He saying?

Jesus, thank you for choosing me. Thank you for loving me enough to leave paradise, just to bring me Home. I don't always feel chosen or favoured. And I sometimes battle disbelief and fear. Can you help me, Jesus? Help me to live as the person You have chosen. Help me to see myself through Your eyes, and keep my heart and mind fixed on You as You walk me deeper into my purpose. Amen.

CHAPTER 15

The Problem of Staying Stuck

"Of one thing I am perfectly sure; God's story never ends with ashes."
—Elisabeth Elliot

My face-first freefall resulted in a messy belly flop that not only took my breath away, but it shook me at the very core. It's not easy, this journey through the valley of rejection.

Lysa TeKeurst said it perfectly when she told her readers, "I licked the floor of hell."[8] I get this picture, and I'm thinking you do too. Rejection and its co-accusers can level us, and if we aren't diligent and determined, we will remain facedown, licking the floor, stuck forever. Moving through the valley of pain requires a choice. A decision to reject the limiting labels we have collected and to accept the life-giving labels God gives us.

> Your bottom of the valley is God's workbench. Your distress call prompts Him to action.

Your bottom of the valley is God's workbench. Your distress call prompts Him to action. The Bible is full of examples of God attending to the needs of His kids and responding to our distress calls. Psalm 107:19 says, "*Then they cried to the LORD in their trouble, and He saved them from their distress.*"

Isaiah 41:13 tells us, *"For I am the LORD your God who takes hold of your right hand, and says to you, 'Do not fear; I will help you.'"*

Daniel 6:27 reminds, *"He rescues and he saves; he performs signs and wonders in the heavens and on the earth. He has rescued Daniel from the power of the lions."*

Accepting the rescue, making the choice to move forward in God's plan, and embracing your new identity and the new name He has for you—it's a decision. It is never God's plan for us to stay stuck in the valley. He may allow us to wander through it for a bit, because He has things to teach us, but His heart's desire is for us to walk in freedom.

Shame and the Rearview Mirror

Remember Wendy—the woman I met through the meal slot of her isolation cell? The unhealed wounds of her past drew her into harmful choices, and these actions led to a shame story she couldn't escape and a prison sentence that stole her hope. I understood Wendy—maybe you do too.

The shame story that threatened my life and the one that may be threatening yours holds nothing good in store for us. It does not have our best interest at heart, nor does it want us to believe there is goodness ahead. Shame is a past-focused bully, rehearsing mistakes, replaying traumas, and reciting wrongs.

> Shame is a past-focused bully, rehearsing mistakes, replaying traumas, and reciting wrongs.

Wendy carried shame like a heavy blanket over her shoulders, and I can't deny that I have too. I understand the fear of moving forward because of the rejection story in my life. Like Wendy's prison gate experience, I felt certain I wasn't deserving of freedom and terrified that maybe the words said to me and the narrative that haunted me was all true.

But shame does not get to sentence us to a life in shackles. We do not serve a God Who is focused on the past. We serve the present and future-focused God who declares us worthy of His love and is determined to release us from the past. Wendy struggled to understand this.

> Shame does not get to sentence us to a life in shackles.

We eventually did get Wendy to her new community and the reintegration team was exceptional at helping her in her new life. The release plan was effective, and Wendy enjoyed success for almost a year in her new community. She held a job that was meaningful to her, developed relationships, and was saving for a vehicle. But unfortunately, freedom can be hard. Shame is an expert at reciting old narratives and drawing us into unhealthy patterns. Wendy spent the next several years battling freedom. For most of her life, Wendy had accepted an identity not meant for her. Handed down from abusive authority figures, confirmed time and time again by a system that was more interested in detaining her than in helping her heal, she wrestled old demons. She accepted this hand-me-down identity as her truth, and when that happened, she began to live according to that identity.

Over the next several years, Wendy cycled through the correctional system before she found herself with a lengthy sentence in a federal institution. At the time of this writing, Wendy lives in a small concrete cell awaiting another release, another chance at freedom.

Prior to her last sentencing, Wendy sent me a short message that read, "Thank you for believing in me. For a few months I thought I could do it. Like I said, women like me don't walk free."

Wrestling with labels was debilitating for Wendy. Her identity was so connected to her past that she was unable to move forward in freedom. Subconsciously, or maybe even consciously, Wendy decided the abuse and pain-informed choices that brought her to jail somehow had the final say about who she was. She was blinded to the fact that she didn't deserve either.

The old labels limited Wendy from seeing her potential and believing she could enjoy a new life. Accepting freedom was so far outside of this imposed identity that she couldn't find her footing in it. Wendy was stuck in a story that held her hostage in the past. Even those months when she was living in freedom weren't enough. She felt the tug to look back and return to a life she believed she deserved. Maybe you can see yourself in Wendy's story. I know I can. I've wrestled with the choice to accept release and embrace the new, or to stand at the gate, shackled by the past, believing the narrative that declares me unworthy, unlovable, and unable.

I've stood where Wendy stood, and I've wondered if maybe women like me don't walk free.

The Tricky Tactic of Rewriting History

Rejection offers a unique experience with loss and pain. Grief is a normal and necessary part of the recovery process when we have lost someone, but rejection doesn't allow for pure grieving. Rejection taints grief with shame. The arsenal of co-accusers holds us hostage to the critical narrative that spins stories about us in our minds. And while we grieve the loss, we also come to believe the loss is related to some deep-seated inadequacy in us.

This idea of releasing the past and accepting freedom can seem like an impossible task when we're tormented with anxiety, shame and insecurity. If I'm being honest, I actually scoffed at the idea of possibly releasing the past and working through or beyond what seemed to paralyze me. This part of the journey had me in a totally different type of wrestle with God. How do we let go of the past and move forward?

There were a number of things that seemed to keep me stuck. I carried a weight that pushed me down and took my breath away. And there was another thing happening in that emotional quicksand.

The rejection narrative seemed to be rewriting history in my mind, highlighting the happy times, taunting me with them. This highlight reel showed me what I had lost, rubbed my nose in it constantly, and then criticized me for losing it. In this stuck state, I found myself glorifying the past, longing for it, even bartering with God. The more I longed for the old, the bigger and heavier my inner labels became, and the deeper I sunk into the quicksand that was keeping me from freedom. Staring longingly at the past is not a new problem.

If you're familiar with the biblical account of Lot in Genesis 19, you will remember that Mrs. Lot was given a chance at freedom. She lived in one of the two most corrupt cities of the day, Sodom and Gomorrah. Through a convincing conversation with Abram, God agreed to spare Sodom and Gomorrah if even ten righteous people could be found. We know how this went.

The angels were sent to help get Lot, his wife, and their two daughters out of the town before God destroyed it. His direction was clear, "Hurry and don't look back."

But Mrs. Lot couldn't help herself, could she? Genesis 19:26 tells us, *"But Lot's wife looked back, and she became a pillar of salt."*

We don't know why she looked back. Was she curious about what God would do? Did she forget something important? Could she hear the voices of her friends and want one more look at the city she called home?

Given what I have learned in my own grieving, I think it's very possible that Mrs. Lot was heartbroken and shocked that this was actually happening. The life she had come to love was over. Memories of dinner parties, walks in the park, and times of closeness with people she loved were held in that city. And while there was tremendous brokenness behind those city walls, a part of her was also left there. Looking back for Mrs. Lot, while disobedient, may have been rooted in grief and longing for the familiar and precious bits and pieces that were her life. I didn't always understand this possibility.

As a teenager, I snubbed my nose at Mrs. Lot, rolling my eyes at her disobedience. It seemed easy to condemn this woman from my privileged thirteen-year-old position. Life hadn't yet called me into the valley. I stood on a comfortable platform, declaring her rebellious and ungrateful, even deserving of her fate. From my perspective, firmly situated in my summer-camp, family-holiday good life, I judged Mrs. Lot for making the fatal error of looking back. But not anymore.

I now get why Mrs. Lot looked back—it was familiar. And despite Sodom and Gomorrah's spiritual darkness, I imagine there were things there she loved and people she felt close to. The past holds pain *and* pleasure. That's why we grieve. That's why we look back. It's human nature to reminisce and hash over the previous. Within that, we may find ourselves glorifying what is gone.

Rearview Mirrors Hold No Promise

God is present-future focused, not present-past focused. He calls us to keep our eyes on Him, even when our former lives call us to look back. Isaiah 43:18–19 says, *"Forget the former things; do not dwell on the past. See, I am doing a new thing! Now it springs up; do you not perceive it? I am making a way in the wilderness and streams in the wasteland."*

God wants us to allow Him to lead us out of things not meant for us and toward Him. Sometimes this is terrifying, and our human instinct is to let our thoughts rush back to the familiar. But our present-future focused God wants all of our attention. Eyes up, ears and heart open, moving into His plan.

We can learn a lot from Mrs. Lot, and I'd like to suggest we also learn much from Wendy. Both were stuck. Both women felt ill-equipped to walk away from what had hurt them, so they could move forward in freedom when they were given the opportunity. Their identities were connected to their former lives. That's human.

The labels these women carried created an identity that was familiar to them. When disaster struck and tragedy took away all they knew, they were left with an opportunity to make a new life and accept new labels. But neither of them did that, and there was a time I didn't think I could either.

While the valley offers some very deep quicksand, it also holds the richest soil. The bottom of a valley can hold us back, keep us stuck, and limit our God-given potential. Or it can present a unique opportunity to hear our Heavenly Father's voice and accept His life-giving labels, allowing Him to turn us back around and face us forward. He will lead us through if we let Him. We get to choose.

KEY TAKEAWAYS

- Moving through the valley of rejection is a choice.

- We can accept limiting labels or life-giving labels.

- Being stuck can result from belief in labels from our past or from looking back longingly at the familiar.

- God is present-future focused, not present-past focused.

- Moving forward in God's plan is an act of obedience and trust.

- The labels thrust on us create an identity that can get in the way of God's plan for us.

REJECTION RECOVERY

For the LORD your God is living among you, He is a mighty savior. He will take delight in you with gladness. With his love, he will calm all your fears. He will rejoice over you with joyful songs (Zephaniah 3:17 NLT).

THERAPEUTIC QUESTIONS

- If the limiting labels holding you hostage had a plan for your life, what would it be?

- If you are standing in quicksand right now, what one action would help you reach toward solid, fertile soil?

- There is a story you're going to tell about these days in the valley. What do you want to be able to say about yourself?

- What new labels might be awaiting you? And how might these help you take those first steps out of stuckness, toward freedom?

JOURNAL PROMPT

Set a timer for five minutes and write out your thoughts and feelings about this quote. "And the day came when the risk to remain tight in a bud was greater than the risk to bloom." –Author unknown

Dear Jesus, thank you for not leaving me alone in this valley. I know You want more for me than this. I'm struggling to let go of my past and the labels I've accepted as truth about me. Sometimes I really miss the familiar people and places I used to call friends, family, and home. I don't want to be stuck gazing back into those places not meant for me. Help me trust You and move forward when you ask me to. Your plans are better, and I want to have faith in You alone through this time. Help me keep my eyes fixed on You. Amen.

PART 4

Roadblocks and Reminders

CHAPTER 16

The Temptation of Revenge

"A man that studieth revenge keeps his own wounds green."

—Francis Bacon

Let me introduce you to Alice and her wrestle with revenge. Shortly after their nineteenth anniversary, her husband had announced the end and moved into the spare room. In those excruciatingly slow-moving moments, on the heels of his decision, Alice was living in thick, merciless quicksand—stuck in the pain, gripped with despair.

It was as though something had wrapped its deadly fingers around her neck, and every breath might be Alice's last. His absence in bed that first night was agonizing, but what pained her more was hearing him in the next room, watching sitcoms–unphased by her brokenness.

For many days, Alice endured what she referred to as "his cruel indifference," while he slipped out to work before she woke, and then came home hours after she went to bed. The only evidence of his homecoming was his laughter in the spare room beside her.

It became unbearable for Alice to be in the same home as the man she loved. Living so separately and experiencing such rejection felt impossible. In desperation, and as an act of self-care, Alice asked him to leave for a week. She planned to use the time to pack up her things and find an apartment. He agreed. The next morning, he was gone.

Her mom flew in, girlfriends showed up, and with heaviness she had no words for, she sorted through and packed up two decades of her life. For months prior, Alice had begged and pleaded with her husband to stay. Behaviours that seemed to push him away further. She left love notes all over the house and she had prayed—constantly. But his eyes told the story of a man long gone.

There was evidence of a secret life, but Alice believed God would bring him out of that. His choices meant a heartbreaking ripple effect for not just Alice, but their daughters, their families, and friends. Still, she knew God was able to bring beauty from ashes. She believed for a miraculous healing, and she declared God's promises.

But the miracle she was praying for didn't come. The beauty Alice thought God should bring from the ashes was not in His will for her. And as the days passed, big, ugly emotions were knocking at the door of her heart. Fending off despair, disbelief, anxiety, and anger became a daily battle, and this roller coaster was a minute-by-minute ride she didn't think she could survive.

Wrestling with anger had Alice reciting revenge fantasies in her mind. In her pain and her humanness, she entertained the idea of retaliation—she wanted him to hurt too. This valley was dark, and anger had a stranglehold she had never felt before.

> Even when things are very bad, God is still very good.

Even when things are very bad, God is still very good. But when you're face down on the valley floor, and all the grossness of the injustice and pain is swirling around you, God's goodness can be hard to see. Alice found herself questioning God. But more than that, she wondered if He would serve up the consequences she thought were deserved.

The revenge-focused spin cycle filled many days, and the more time she spent plotting retaliation, the further she felt from Jesus. And the less hope she felt in the valley.

Alice wrestled hard, but God in His grace, wrestled back. While the desire for revenge is human nature, we are not called to give in to our human naturedness.

Revenge and trusting God don't go hand in hand. Alice had to choose one or the other. Giving up control of consequences is a painfully difficult, but absolutely necessary step on the quest for healing.

But how? How do we step in the direction of healing when the need for revenge keeps us plotting payback scenarios?

As I fumbled my way through the revenge-focused season of my valley, I landed on a three-part process to help me move away from vengeance toward restoration:

1. Release: This is a difficult step, but necessary for healing. It's about trusting our Heavenly Father with the consequences He thinks are appropriate. These consequences may look different than what we would like, but when we release revenge to Him, it's His to do with what He sees fit.

    It occurred to me that God was equally (okay, likely more) upset about my marriage than I was. He was angry too—and hurt. And His compassionate heartache for me through the valley was evidenced in how He showed up and travelled every painful step with me.

Please remember this, God has not forgotten about you. What happened is not lost on Him. When we release the need for revenge to Him, we free Him up to take care of the outcomes. We make room for the healing work He wants to do in our lives.

2. Reframe: I've learned that when wrestling strong emotions in this valley, it's helpful to reframe things by becoming students or researchers of our experience. This creates distance from the pain and provides a different lens through which to view the situation.

There are many ways to do this, but if you're feeling creative today, try a narrative therapy exercise. Mentally pull yourself back from the idea of revenge and picture it *over there* (some people picture it in a corner or on a chair) and then bring healing into the room.

How does this interaction go? What does healing say to revenge?

If your conversation goes at all like mine did, revenge will try to convince you it promotes healing. It wants us to believe that seeking retaliation will make us feel better, that causing pain in the other person will bring about our recovery.

Look at revenge as an obstacle to healing. Entertaining thoughts of revenge will become stumbling blocks in your recovery and take you off course in this process.

If you were in my office, I'd encourage you to put revenge in a chair on the other side of the room. And then I'd interview you by asking the following questions:

- What does revenge ultimately want for you?
- If revenge had its way, what would it do?
- Does revenge want to grow you up toward the person you want to be? Or down and away from her/him?
- Is that okay with you?
- Is revenge looking out for your best interest?
- Is revenge interested in helping you be closer to Jesus or further from Him?
- If revenge is invited into your life and given the reins, what might happen to you, your peace, your reputation, or your legacy?
- What has the thoughts of revenge taken from you that you'd like back?
- What does healing have to say in this situation?
- How would things look differently if you focused solely on healing and resisted the pull of revenge?

3. Resist: This was the hardest one for me. There is something about the idea of revenge that feels very satisfying to me. I found myself allowing old thoughts of retaliation, and reciting spiteful monologues in my head. But when I ruminated on the wounded thinking of retaliation and revenge, I felt an increase in anxiety and a distance from Jesus. Resisting the urge to think about revenge, or behave in a vengeful way made room for peace—which is what I craved more than anything.

It's Not About Just Desserts

If you're like me, there is a significant push-pull here. Wanting payback is a normal human response to an injustice and wrongdoing. The desire for revenge can recruit a person for days or years, even a lifetime if left unhealed. In some cases, revenge becomes contagious, absorbing others into the "just desserts" mindset. It is normal to entertain thoughts of revenge when we've been hurt. The Bible holds countless examples of God-fearing, God-loving people who battled this very problem. I can only assume Paul preached against revenge because it was a problem in his day too.

In Romans 12:19, he reminds us: *"Beloved, never avenge yourselves, but leave it to the wrath of God, for it is written 'Vengeance is mine, I will repay,' says the Lord"* (ESV).

In Ephesians 4:31–32, *"Let all bitterness and wrath and anger and clamor and slander be put away from you, along with all malice. Be kind to one another, tender hearted, forgiving one another, as God in Christ forgave you"* (ESV).

The Bible is clear—revenge is God's business. Instead, we must pursue mercy and forgiveness. In her devotions one morning, God reminded Alice of a promise she had made months earlier when she began to notice the unravelling of her relationship. She had promised God that no matter what happened in her marriage, she would lead with love. Her heart's desire was to make Jesus proud of her. But, as she faced ongoing rejection by her husband and navigated the painful twists and turns of the valley, she had lost sight of this promise.

Revenge was becoming an option for Alice, and she needed loving intervention from her Heavenly Father. In His gentle way, He directed her thoughts back to His promise in Proverbs 20:22.

"*Do not say, 'I will repay evil'; wait for the LORD, and he will deliver you*" (ESV).

This is one of the hardest parts of a Christ-centred life. The battle is real between our human-natured desire for revenge and that deep knowing that Jesus is asking us to leave vengeance to Him. The very clear message on Alice's heart was to love her husband well, even in the pain. Even though he didn't *deserve* it. She was being asked by her Heavenly Father to do the opposite of her human nature.

In our humanness we want revenge, but God requires obedience to Him. We cannot act according to our sin-nature while at the same time be in line with God's plan for our lives and ask Him to bless us. We have to choose. Obedience is especially difficult when we desperately want to do things our own way.

Let me assure you, Alice wrestled with God. She pushed hard and was very concerned that God was not going to do what she thought He should do—severely punish the one who hurt her. Some wounded part of her worried that letting go of revenge would move her further from her husband. Holding on to the anger seemed weirdly intimate. It was through many conversations with prayer partners, family, counselors, and God Himself, that she was able to stand down and take herself off the case for revenge.

Letting go of her payback fantasies did not mean what had happened to Alice was okay or even tolerable. It wasn't. Letting go of ideas of retaliation did not suggest her husband was right to do what he did. He wasn't.

But pursuing holiness over rightness needed to become her focus. Releasing the anger and the desire for revenge meant Alice was willing to move forward with God. Vengeance and retaliation thinking keep us trapped in the pain and connected to the offender in a toxic, pain- induced intimacy. It is the literal quicksand in the valley of rejection, and every single time it holds us back from who God is calling us to be. Entertaining thoughts of revenge cannot facilitate healing.

Alice's decision to trust God to be Who He says He is and allow Him to be in charge of any potential consequences took her off the case for revenge. Turning the outcome over to Him meant Alice was no longer responsible for justice. And it allowed freedom to work toward forgiveness—the thing she didn't want to do. But she knew this was the next important step in her relationship with Jesus. It was with this very pivotal decision that things in the valley changed.

The Struggle Is Real

I am not suggesting this is easy, not at all. Please know this may very well be the most difficult part of the journey for you. But until you let go of the desire for revenge and trust God with this, you will not be free to continue the healing process He is calling you to.

Alice decided to leave justice with Jesus. On the heels of that decision, freedom rushed in and took the place of revenge. The difficult decision to let go of thoughts of retaliation made way for love and even compassion. It felt like a miracle as Alice held up her hands and released the anger to Jesus. At first, she admits there was reluctance and even doubt. This was hard, and she told Him so. The prayer of her heart was to be obedient and to make Jesus proud of her. And she told Him that too. She could almost picture Him reaching out to her and with a smile of compassion on His face, taking the anger. Taking her need for retribution. Taking her husband.

With revenge gone, love and compassion came back strong. The miracle Alice had prayed for happened—but not in the way she thought it would. She felt a need to bless her husband, not harm him. Alice wanted to show him love despite his choices. And as crazy as this sounds, she set to work making his favorite meals. Not as a way to manipulate him or make him feel guilty, but to show kindness. She wanted him to receive a very clear message: *Regardless of what has happened, I love you.*

She left the meals in the fridge along with some fresh groceries. As the movers carried out the last bits and pieces of her furniture, she was aware of the co-existence of some very opposing emotions. The pain was still intense, and there was still shock and confusion. Her heart was still broken and the future uncertain. But the need for revenge was gone. And in its place stood hope. She felt gratitude for the life well lived in that home. In her heart, she could feel a level of contentment, even joy, that she still couldn't fully explain.

The quicksand of the valley threatens to keep us captive in the humanness of hardship. God's goodness doesn't change based on our circumstances, and the healing He holds for us is only restricted by our choices. Giving revenge fantasies over to Jesus is an important choice-point in our journey through the valley, but it doesn't necessarily mean things go smoothly all the time.

> God's goodness doesn't change based on our circumstances, and the healing He holds for us is only restricted by our choices.

We learn a lot about people at the end of relationships. How people navigate injustice, wrongness and pain says a lot about them. You and I have been wounded by someone, and perhaps their sin has opened deep pain that leaves us wanting revenge. But let's not allow their mistakes to drag us into choices and behaviours in conflict with who God is calling us to be.

Alice's testimony of love in the face of rejection reached the heart of many women in her life. She was asked to speak at her church, guest blog about forgiveness in the face of injustice, and perhaps most significantly, those friends in her life who didn't know Jesus were struck by her ability to show such love. While she was encouraged to retaliate and tempted to seek revenge, her kindness spoke volumes to those around her.

> This understanding of God's goodness allows us to let ourselves off the hook for rolling out revenge when we have been wronged.

This wrestle between holiness and rightness is ongoing. When we understand God's deep desire for closeness with us and when we see Him as a loving, protective and just Father, we gain clarity about our circumstances. This understanding of God's goodness allows us to let ourselves off the hook for rolling out revenge when we have been wronged. Moving away from a payback mindset makes way for the beautiful life He wants to bless us with.

KEY TAKEAWAYS

- Wanting revenge is a natural response to wrongdoing or injustice.

- Pursuing holiness must trump our pursuit of rightness and revenge.

- Letting go of the revenge mindset is a choice. And this choice makes way for closeness with God and freedom from toxic and unhealthy emotions.

- God wants us to leave vengeance with him.

- Revenge and healing cannot co-exist.

REJECTION RECOVERY

> Never pay back evil with more evil. Do things in such a way that everyone can see you are honorable. Do all that you can to live in peace with everyone. Dear friends, never take revenge. Leave that to the righteous anger of God. For the Scriptures say, "I will take revenge; I will pay them back," says the LORD (Romans 12:17–19 NLT).

THERAPEUTIC QUESTIONS

- What does revenge have you thinking about?
- How would things feel differently if vengeful thoughts weren't present?
- What would you like to have stand in the place of vengeance? Why is that preferred?
- What needs to happen to turn control of revenge over to Jesus?

JOURNAL PROMPT

One day you will tell a story about how you have travelled this season of your life. What is the story you want to be able to tell?

Dear Jesus, I am struggling with thoughts of revenge. I want _____ to hurt too. But I know this is not what you want for me. You want me to turn it over to you and let you handle consequences. Please help me trust you with this, and please heal me from this human tendency to seek payback. I want peace and love to lead, not revenge. Thank you for your grace and patience with me through this. Amen.

CHAPTER 17

Forgiveness

The Chapter I'm Scared to Write

"You'll never learn how strong your heart is until you learn to forgive who broke it."

—Anonymous

You get a standing ovation. If you're still reading, I applaud you. I would have skipped this chapter at certain points in my recovery journey. I have heard it said, "Unforgiveness is like drinking poison and expecting the other person to die." Or "Forgiveness is a gift you give yourself."

My younger self is rolling her eyes. *Bunk!* She says in her head.

I decided those quotes came from the inexperienced, gravy-train riders. Free of abandonment, deception, or serious injustice, knowing little about forgiveness, these cake-walking do-gooders with no business advising on forgiveness—they're the ones writing those quotes.

To say I was resistant to forgiveness is an understatement.

The wheels of my recovery came to a grinding halt at this junction. To forgive or not forgive? You can probably imagine how this went for me. It was an emotional standoff with God, and on any given day, I would offer Him countless reasons why forgiveness was out of the question.

In fact, I said *No*. I told God *No*.

Whoopsie.

My journal from those days shows the wrestle. To give you a summary of my year-long, push-pull with forgiveness, here is why I struggled:

1. I didn't want to forgive. Plain and simple. The wrongness was too wrong. The injustice was too unjust. And I didn't want to let it go. I just didn't. I was a victim of a very bad thing, and in some weird way, being a victim was kind of satisfying. To forgive meant I had to give that up.

2. Forgiveness was not deserved. Guilty people should pay for their mistakes. And I had determined that what had happened was undeserving of forgiveness.

3. I wanted to protect and honor my pain. The depth of brokenness from the rejection seemed worthy of holding a grudge. To forgive felt devaluing of my wound and in my opinion, it communicated my agreement with the choices leading to the breakdown of our family.

4. I wanted justice and validation. Somewhere along the line, I decided forgiving would suggest acceptance of the wrongness and let my former spouse off the hook for what he had done. And this would mean he wouldn't pay. And that just didn't seem fair to me.

5. I feared that forgiveness would make me vulnerable to further injustices. Unforgiveness felt like a good defense against future pain.

6. I deserved to be angry and forgiveness felt like letting go of what I deserved and letting him off the hook for what I believed he deserved.

I Was Wrong

But I was wrong about forgiveness. I misunderstood what God was asking me to do. Forgiveness is not about what is deserving or not deserving. It does not deny the existence of pain or the fact that something wrong has occurred. It is not a declaration of agreement, nor does it affirm the wrongdoing.

Had something very wrong taken place? Yes.

Was I deserving of betrayal, abandonment, and rejection? No.

Would I have liked punishment and justice to be unleashed with a fury? Oh, yes.

But, was holding unforgiveness going to make any of that better? Not even a little bit.

My holding unforgiveness did not impact anyone but me. In fact, the longer and tighter I embraced unforgiveness, the thicker and grosser my bitterness got. Choosing unforgiveness meant I was inadvertently aligning myself with resentment. And if I've learned anything over my years as a therapist, it's that resentment is poison.

> Choosing unforgiveness meant I was inadvertently aligning myself with resentment.

I've dabbled in it during seasons of my life and bitterness never goes well. Catherine Ponder says, "When you hold resentment toward another, you are bound to that person or condition by an emotional link that is stronger than steel. Forgiveness is the only way to dissolve that link and get free."[9]

Pivot.

I felt bound to this injury—this betrayal and rejection. And the resentment building as a result of my unforgiveness had me reciting rage fantasies in my mind that kept me awake at night. I wanted freedom, but I felt stuck.

When the topic of forgiveness is brought up in counseling—usually by me—clients often shake their heads. I get this anti-forgiveness, head shaking. If my head wasn't attached, it would have spun off several times through my own fight with forgiveness.

What gets in the way of forgiveness? Exploring the obstacles with women in my life, I found the top three hurdles to forgiveness are:

1. Pride and ego—it's as sharp for me to write as it is for you to read. Believe me, this isn't easy to say. It's hard to tell people that pride is the obstacle to forgiveness, but in all honesty, it's the thing that shows up most. The wounds we feel because of the things done to us breed resentment. That resentment evokes an "Absolutely not! Are you kidding me!? Not a chance," hands on hips, head shaking, incensed response. Pride tag-teams with ego, and together they inform the anti-forgiveness perspective, standing as barricades to healing.

2. Ongoing wounds inflicted by the offender leave us under constant assault. Forgiveness is especially difficult when we are in contact with the person who has rejected and wounded us. In my forgiveness work, I decided to hold very strong boundaries in place and ended all contact. This eliminated the opportunity to hurt me further and made space for my healing. But not everyone has that luxury. If you must maintain contact with the one who has rejected you, forgiveness becomes a day-to-day activity, making it exhausting and especially difficult to release.

3. Misunderstanding forgiveness and what it requires of us, we decide we know what forgiveness is, and then we base our choices on those misunderstandings.

The Truth of the Matter

But what if forgiveness isn't what you think it is? Over the years, I have counselled hundreds of women struggling with unforgiveness. Below is a list of myths and truths collected from several years of personal and professional conversations about forgiveness:

Myth about Forgiviness	Truth about Forgivness
Forgiving means forgetting.	You are not asked to forget. In fact, as humans, we cannot decide to forget something. But forgiveness makes way for such healing that the acute memory fades and the negative emotion attached to the incident often disappears. This leads to more of an indifference, rather than a forgetting.
I will have to be in relationship with that person again.	You get to choose who to be in relationship with. Forgiveness does not mean you have to reconcile.
Forgiveness is about the other person. It's a nice gesture or act of kindness to them.	Forgiveness is about you. It's a gift you give yourself and has nothing to do with the person who has wronged you.
Forgiveness happens immediately when I decide to forgive.	Forgiveness is a process. It takes time.
If I forgive, it says I agree with, approve of, or support the person's actions	Forgiveness is a bold act against the wrong done to you. It's an act of rebellion against the pain. And it does not communicate agreement or approval.
If I forgive, I become a doormat, open to more mistreatment.	Forgiveness offers you a fresh lens to help you better understand yourself and build boundaries, it makes way for a new screening process.

Myth about Forgiviness	Truth about Forgivness
If I forgive, it won't hurt anymore.	Forgiveness makes way for healing, and the pain will lessen as we move forward in forgiveness.
Forgiveness is a feeling. To forgive, I must feel forgiving	Forgiveness is an act of the will and a process. We don't need to feel anything to forgive.
Once I make the decision to forgive, its smooth sailing	The decision to forgive marks a pivot point and the beginning of a process. You may need to forgive over and over again.

Lysa Terkeurst's book, *Forgiving What You Can't Forget*, says, "Me not forgiving the people who hurt me was agreeing to bring the hurt they caused into every present-day situation I was in—hurting me over and over and over again. Holding on to this hurt wasn't diminishing my pain. It was multiplying it. And it was manipulating me to become someone I didn't want to be. So, instead of making anything right, it was just making everything even more wrong—me, them, the whole situation."[10]

I just want to stand and clap for Lysa's oh-so important message here. Unforgiveness doesn't make anything right, it just makes more wrong.

Forgiveness is an act of obedience. But if I'm completely honest, that wasn't the part that tipped me over into agreement with God. I want it to be. I want to be that woman who says, *I forgive because God requires it of me. I want to be obedient to Him.* I admire those who say that. But for me, it was about something different.

The valley of rejection had given me an up close and personal experience with Jesus. He had led me through the most difficult season of my life, and His kindness to me was unlike anything I had ever known. Through the tiny details of perfect parking spaces at my new apartment and the kindness of strangers, He whispered His care for me. And in the mountain moving moments, He bellowed His unconditional and immoveable determination to love me and bring me back in line with His plan. I grew to appreciate Him very much.

And I did not want to hurt His feelings.

Unforgiveness hurts the One I love.

Coming to this new understanding of forgiveness was a process. I pictured sitting down over coffee with Jesus, explaining why I had chosen unforgiveness, pointing to all of the reasons for holding anger and resentment toward the person who had hurt me.

In this coffee conversation with Jesus, I reminded Him about the betrayal and rejection—as if He had forgotten. I declared myself deserving of justice for the wrongs done to me. And I told Him I would forgive everything else, but not this one thing.

And then, I pictured His face. And, I pictured His eyes.

It's at this point in the conversation, Jesus reminded me about the rejection and betrayal He had faced during His time here. The many people He trusted and did life with, who turned away from Him, sold Him out, and did the unthinkable. And then He reminded me of the countless rejections He faces every day, even now, by those He loves, the children He died for. Including me.

My sin is active rejection of Him. Unforgiveness recruits me into alliance with those who disregard Jesus.

And so, I decided to forgive. This act of love for Jesus and obedience to Him was a declaration of my trust and commitment to Him. I did not forgive because it was deserving. None of us is deserving of forgiveness. We forgive because we love Jesus and He asks us to. And in this process came the decision to allow Him to roll out any consequences He thought were necessary. I took myself off the case.

> I did not forgive because it was deserving. None of us is deserving of forgiveness. We forgive because we love Jesus and He asks us to.

A Hypothetical Scenario

Maybe you're where I was, toying with the possibility of forgiveness. I admit to you, I grumbled my way to the edge of this decision and then teetered there for a long time. You're in good company if you are snubbing your nose.

So, easy does it, but hypothetically speaking, if one makes the decision to forgive, exactly how does one go about doing it? Here's a few ideas to get you started:

1. Invite Jesus into the process and rely on Him throughout. This can be as simple as, "Okay God, here we go. I don't know how to do this, and I don't even know that I want to, but I'm working toward forgiving. Can you help me with this?"

2. Acknowledge your emotions and speak the pain. Identifying hurt is an important first step. "This person hurt me deeply. My heart is broken. I hate how this feels. I am angry. I'm terrified." You may need to find an emotions chart somewhere to help recognize what you're feeling, but this is essential to healing.

3. Release your grip. Actively let go of the wrong done to you and the person you're trying to forgive. Picture yourself releasing it, giving it to God and being free from it.

4. Remember the forgiveness you've been given. Take a moment to write down all the things God has forgiven you for. He actively chooses to forgive us and when we reflect back on what He has done, it seems fitting that we would do the same.

5. Pray for the person who has hurt you. It's hard to be angry at someone we are praying for. Pray every single time you think of that person, pray for their salvation or their healing. This is a hard one, for sure. But it is essential in the forgiving process.

Maybe you're nodding your head here. You get the importance of forgiving the person who has rejected or betrayed you, and you are well on your way through this process. But, like many of us, you get hung up on the idea of self-forgiveness.

> Your pain is part of your story, but it is not the point of your story.

I understand the struggle. Your pain is part of your story, but it is not the point of your story. And, if no one has told you this, your past does not need to travel any further on your journey. This is where it gets dropped off.

Rejection and shame burden us with the difficult task of forgiving ourselves. You may have fought like crazy to salvage the relationship. I did. You may have done your very best. I did.

But still, the relationship failed.

And, since we're human, you've probably made mistakes in your relationship. Me too. And maybe there are things you wish you had done differently. Wow, me too.

The *what ifs*, *shoulds* and *shouldn't haves* haunt us. We could *should* ourselves to death. But regret keeps us linked to the past, and as we have worked our way through and into this new chapter of our lives, it's time to cut those ties.

> The *what ifs*, *shoulds* and *shouldn't haves* haunt us. We could *should* ourselves to death.

While learning from our mistakes can inform our choices in the future, holding regrets keeps us unhealthily attached to them.

As I wrestled with this part of my journey, I worked through a three-part process to help with self-forgiveness:

1. Admit the sin, shame, and regrets to God. Tell Him everything you are holding onto. I found that making an itemized list helped me with this.
2. Ask for His forgiveness. Go through each item, each sin, each regret and ask Him to take it from you. Ask Him to cleanse you from the past.
3. Determine to accept forgiveness and agree with God that His Son's death on the cross was enough to free you from your past.

Regret informs shame. When we hold unforgiveness toward ourselves, clinging to regrets, we fan the flames of shame. I know I've said this before, but I think it bears repeating: to hold unforgiveness and shame means we disagree with God that His Son's death was enough.

> To hold unforgiveness and shame means we disagree with God that His Son's death was enough.

Jesus died for you. He had you on His mind when He chose to live as a man, and He had you on His heart as He died a brutal death on the cross. And because of His life, His death, and His resurrection, we can walk away from our past toward the incredible future He has for us. The cross gives us peace and His resurrection gives us hope. Let's decide to agree with Him. Forgiving the wrongs others have done to us and refusing to hold unforgiveness for ourselves brings freedom. And more than that, it brings us closer to Jesus. Tucked up close to Him is exactly where we find the freedom to be who He created us to be.

KEY TAKEAWAYS

- Forgiveness is a process.

- Forgiving someone does not communicate agreement or approval of the wrong.

- Forgiving is an act of obedience but also a declaration of our love for Jesus.

- Unforgiveness breeds resentment and acts as poison in our lives.

- Self-forgiveness is a decision to accept what God says is true of you.

- Your pain is part of your story, but it's not the point of your story.

- Unforgiving ourselves breeds regret and shame and keeps us from the freedom God calls us to.

REJECTION RECOVERY

For if you forgive other people when they sin against you, your heavenly Father will also forgive you (Matthew 6:14).

THERAPEUTIC QUESTIONS

- What obstacles stand in the way of you forgiving him/her/them?

- If these obstacles weren't in place, what would you do?

- Forgiveness is a bold stand against the pain. What else does it stand against?

- Forgiving ourselves communicates agreement with God that sending His Son to die was enough. Picture yourself over coffee with Him. How would that conversation go?

JOURNAL PROMPT

Interview your one-year older self, the person who has done the forgiving. What does she tell you about her new life and living in freedom?

God, I have no idea what it means to live out my faith through forgiveness. I don't know how to heal from the brokenness or to forgive those who have hurt me. I need you for this, because I have no power to do this on my own. The betrayal is too big and the rejection is too painful to fathom forgiveness. But I want to be obedient to You, and I know you can help me. I need your strength, wisdom, and guidance. I surrender control and give you everything. Please help me to forgive and move forward with you. Amen.

CHAPTER 18

Grieving the Loss of the Living

"One of the hardest things you will ever have to do is grieve the loss of a person who is still alive."

—ANONYMOUS

I have had a constant longing while writing this book. A longing to sit in person with you, and talk through this whole experience of rejection and rejection recovery. More than any other, this chapter is the one that I would especially like to address in person. Why? Well, mostly because I very much want you to fully understand my heart in this very sensitive, very important section of your healing. I want you to see my face when I say how sorry I am that you are grieving the loss of someone who has walked away. Your loss is great, and your pain is real. There will be people in your life who don't understand it, or will want to rush you through it. Grieving someone who has walked away is a unique, complex experience, requiring special attention.

While writing this chapter, I found myself launching into grief management strategies. I wanted to get down to the business of helping you through this awful time. But a gentle nudge from our Heavenly Father reminded me that He has to be the starting point for healing. True recovery requires a primary focus on Him. There have been times I've taken God out of certain things in my life— almost deciding for Him what parts of me He gets and sometimes even feeling isolated from Him because I've decided He wouldn't understand my pain.

But this grief is not unfamiliar to our Heavenly Father. He has had loved ones walk away too. Please let that linger for a moment. There is no greater love than what Jesus offers us. His love compelled Him to a brutal death on a cross. And every day the children He died for, turn their backs on Him, declare Him unnecessary, and deny His existence. Having endured loss on a small, human scale, I can't even begin to imagine His pain.

During His time on Earth, Jesus Himself endured significant rejection and loss. Isaiah 53:3 says, *"He was despised and rejected—a man of sorrows and acquainted with deepest grief. We turned our backs on him and looked the other way. He was despised, and we did not care"* (NLT).

Despised and rejected, sorrowful and grieving, fully God and also fully man, our Saviour was very familiar with life in the valley of rejection. He was fully acquainted with grief. And He exposed Himself to this pain so that we could trust Him when He tells us it's going to be okay.

Honouring Your Unique Grief Story

You are uniquely created and your grief story is as individual as you are. God is not surprised by your rejection. And though you may struggle to believe this, He is not angry at you. On the contrary, He is trying to get closer to you. This time of grieving and your season in the valley is offering you intimacy with your Saviour. He cherishes this time with you. It is ridiculously difficult to wrap our heads around, but there is a purpose in our pain, and this complex experience with grief will grow us.

When we accept that our grief is unique to us, and we believe God's promise that He has an individualized plan for each of His

> When we accept that our grief is unique to us, and we believe God's promise that He has an individualized plan for each of His kids, we view our loss as a divine repositioning.

kids, we view our loss as a divine repositioning. We must not get caught up in the comparison game.

We cannot compare grief. Loss is loss, sorrow is sorrow. Losing someone we love impacts our life in a multitude of ways. And because we can never fully know the experience of someone else, we must avoid positioning each other on a hierarchy of loss. Comparison impairs grieving in ourselves and in others. Measuring our experience up against someone else's, robs us and the other person of dignity. By applying our value system to the wound of someone else, we undermine the validity of their pain, while also sabotaging our own true loss experience.

The Grief Recovery Institute suggests the grief you feel will be based mainly on the following factors:

- The absolute uniqueness of your one-of-a-kind relationship with the person.
- The combination of time, intensity, and value the relationship had for you.
- The degree to which you felt emotionally complete, or incomplete, with the person before the end of the relationship, and often for many years prior to that. While the day-to-day conflict may end, it does not complete the unfinished business.[11]

The unique combination of you and your partner is not the same as any other relationship. Within that, your grief is unique and cannot be compared to the grief of another.

We find healing in a compassionate, non-judgemental, comparison-free acceptance of grief.

Grief is deeply complex. And grieving someone who has walked away is especially complicated and confusing. Somehow in our culture we have measured loss and granted it varying levels of respect based on responsibility and fault. We often hold death as the ultimate grief. We measure other losses against it, determining them worthy of greater or lesser respect. Greater or lesser dignity.

Sorrow has also been measured and respected based on fault and responsibility. What assumed influence has impacted your loss? And based on that measure, we give or withhold compassion, respect, and support.

Whether by death or divorce, we relive matrimonial death in waves. Each represents the end of a dream, togetherness, and intimacy. Both are destabilizing and leave us to redefine normal. They end the familiar family home and require a new identity, causing us to move through life differently. Loss is loss.

When we question or try to quantify the grief of others, it casts shadows of suspicion and limits someone's ability to process and heal. And when we measure our own grief or our own process of mourning against that of another, we dishonour our own loss as well as the loss of the other person. Grief is a normal response to losing someone or something you love. It is not saved solely for death. In fact, we grieve many different losses and experience varying levels of bereavement over a large collection of human experiences:

- Divorce or separation
- Loss of health
- Loss of a job
- Death of a pet
- A loved one's serious illness or injury
- A miscarriage
- Our own serious injury, illness, or loss of mobility
- Selling a family home or moving away
- Retirement

What a gift it is to ourselves when we resist judging our grief and the mourning of others. I have never lost a spouse to death or experienced a terrible, life-changing injury or illness. But I do understand sorrow. And even in my unknowing of the particulars of someone's loss, I can absolutely sit in compassion and empathy of shared broken-heartedness.

The Unwanted Gift that Keeps On Giving

Jennifer was deep in grief when she came to my office. After months of high conflict, her husband, whom she adored, asked her to move out. Before she could make sense of what was happening, their tenth anniversary dream trip to Europe had been cancelled and the new vacation-ready outfits returned to the store. Furniture had been divided, and as she stood in the entrance of their family home he handed her a container of family pictures.

Standing this last time in their entrance, she looked at him, begging with her eyes for answers—for understanding. But he was done, and reaching for the door, he said, "Please go. I have things to do."

Confused and heartbroken, Jennifer moved into a basement suite with their two children. Life was different now, in all ways. She had trouble sleeping, because the dreams were intense, and the memories of good times spun through her mind. And there were many, many good times, making her husband's behaviour and his choice to end the relationship so confusing.

Only a month after their separation Jennifer learned he had a girlfriend. Her six-year-old daughter returned home from a visit declaring how nice *Daddy's new friend* was. And, with another breathtaking blow, he was moving her in—into their family home, into the lives of their children.

Her well-meaning friends were incensed, suggesting Jennifer was "better off without him." Reminding her it was "time to move on," and encouraging her to "find someone who would treat her properly."

The conflicting emotions for Jennifer were unrelenting. She missed him and the life they loved together terribly. She could not bear the thought of him sharing a bed and life with another woman, and this new information brought overwhelming grief. Yet, the things he had said over the last year of their marriage wounded her deeply and caused her to question herself and her worth. The conflict, though they tried to keep it from the children, had inevitably impacted the climate in the home and left her feeling tremendous guilt.

This is why grieving a person who has walked away is so complicated. In our grief, we carry memories of the painful and divisive things done and said that were meant to hurt. And then, even after separation, the pain is not left alone to heal. Ongoing conflict, the revelations of secrets, and legal battles with the person we thought would love us forever, add salt to the wounds.

This person, our person, continues to live and breathe, doing their life, often with someone else. In many cases, they rewrite history as a way to influence opinions. And then, as if rushing to the rescue of the reputation of the relationship, the good memories flood in, trying to blot out the broken bits. The confusion this brings is a formidable companion of grief, resulting in an emotional push and pull that feels more like a boxing match than a process of healing.

The grief effect twists and taints good memories for the whole family. Cherished memories no longer evoke happy emotions but become items in the ever-growing list of contaminated moments from the past. Scrapbooks, framed pictures, and family albums are boxed up or thrown away. While the pain softens with time, it rarely makes way for pure reminiscing about these special times in

> Grieving is an ongoing, essential process, requiring intentional effort on our part to manage the rollercoaster of emotions during this season.

the family. Grieving is an ongoing, essential process, requiring intentional effort on our part to manage the rollercoaster of emotions during this season.

Unmanaged grief becomes increasingly difficult to control. I have worked with women so caught up in their grief story that it becomes the defining feature of their lives. Your grief is deep and real, but it does not define you. And staying stuck in the loss will most certainly undermine the healing process you have been working so hard for.

We have the tendency to either run from grief or get stuck in it. Running is an effective temporary avoidance strategy, but when grief catches up, it will tag team anxiety and demand attention. Stuckness, on the other hand, creates a grief-informed lens through which we view other people. It breeds cynicism, separatism, and loneliness—with the potential to keep us imprisoned for a lifetime.

Just Keep Moving

Let's not run from the grieving or stay stuck in it. Instead, let's make the pivotal decision to boldly and courageously face it head on and recognize it as a bridge to the other side. Allowing yourself to grieve. But on the other side, is the ability to fully engage in your life again, with the amazing ability to embrace the freedom that comes from healing.

As you go through this important experience with grief, here are some things to keep in mind, and some suggestions to help you keep moving:

1. Grieving is not a linear process—it does not follow a straight line. The waves of grief will roll in hard some days and feel more gentle on others. Expect the unexpected.
2. Let the feelings come, and then let them go. Feelings are just feelings. They do not need to take up more space or time than necessary.
3. Access a support network and engage in self-care. Grief will want you to isolate. Resist the urge to shrink back. Seek out support and care from others.
4. Give back. Serving others is an integral component of healing from grief. Volunteer at a local shelter, food bank, or any number of places where you can aid others.
5. Be a good researcher. Notice yourself in this experience. Notice the grief and how you are managing it. And be open to meaning making. There is no purposeless pain. Look for God's hands on your life and notice how He is healing you through the pain.
6. Practice acceptance and forgiveness. We may never have all the answers. Huge question marks may dot your story as they do mine. But the sooner you can move in the direction of accepting what was previously unacceptable, and forgive the seemingly unforgivable, the sooner you will feel relief from rejection.

Grieving is lonely and grieving someone who has not died is a confusing and complex experience. You are not alone in this. Look for God in the missing, cry out to Him in your longing for the life and the person you have lost. There has never been a moment you are outside of the watchful eye of your Heavenly Father, and clinging to Him through this season will show you just how much He loves you.

KEY TAKEAWAYS

- Grief is an essential part of healing.
- Grief is a wave-like process and is not linear.
- Jesus understands grief.
- Comparing loss stunts healing and leaves us isolated.
- We are never alone in our grief.

REJECTION RECOVERY

The LORD hears his people when they call to him for help. He rescues them from all their troubles. The LORD is close to the broken hearted; he rescues those whose spirits are crushed (Psalm 34:17-18 NLT).

THERAPEUTIC ACTIVITY

- What acts of comparison are you engaging in that are slowing the grieving process down?

- When you look ahead to your one-year-older self, what does she say about this grieving process?

- How would she encourage you?

- Grieving someone who has not died is especially complicated. How can you honour yourself and this process?

JOURNAL PROMPT

What am I learning about grief that I didn't understand before? And how can I let this learning inform how I show care to others who are experiencing loss in different ways?

Dear Jesus, I am grieving. The loss of this person feels like a wound that may never heal. Some days I can't believe it's real, and the missing is overwhelming. I feel isolated and alone in it, and I have wondered if I'm even allowed to grieve. Please give me courage and strength to travel this confusing and painful time in a way that honours you, and honours the loss. I know You understand rejection, and Your heart hurts with mine. Thank you for comforting me, and for being a safe place to turn to in my grief. Amen.

CHAPTER 19

For the Momma's Heart

"Motherhood is the ultimate call to sacrifice."

—WANGECHI MUTU

She was not quite three years old, and her daddy had left. Confusion and sadness were dark passengers in those early days for my little one, and emotions were very high as she wrestled with the new family dynamic. Meltdowns were a daily occurrence for her at daycare, and the staff had called me in for a meeting. How were we going to help this little girl manage her sorrow?

Motherhood means wearing our heart outside of our bodies for the rest of our lives. It means when bad things happen, we grieve in two realms: one for ourselves, and then with extra venom, we also grieve for our children.

> Motherhood means wearing our heart outside of our bodies for the rest of our lives.

Mom, if you are in that place in your life, grieving the walking away of your partner, and holding the hearts of your children while they grieve, I am so sorry. This is a very hard time for you, and my heart breaks with yours.

As I write this, I'm aware of that oh-so-familiar lump in my throat reminding me that momma's hearts are closely tied. And we are never so vulnerable as when our children are wounded. I see you, and I know this pain. There you are, standing when you want to crumble. Smiling when brokenness threatens to steal your joy. Holding the emotional climate of your home in your weary and shaking hands. All for love. All for the love of those little ones God gave you.

Good for you, Mom. Please hold on. You and your children are going to be okay.

You are not alone in this battle. I stand with you, and more than that, God stands with you. In fact, we know that children are especially loved by Jesus. His word declares Him *Father to the fatherless* (Psalms 68:5 NLT). He is a good Father, and He knows this pain you're facing. His heart breaks with you for your children, and He will absolutely not leave you alone through this time.

How do I know this? I know it with certainty because my daughter and I have travelled through two divorces. And at every turn, without exception, God was with us, showing us His hands in our lives.

My first summer as a single parent was a tough one. Loneliness and fear of the unknown tag-teamed me, causing sleepless nights and emotional days. Having moved across the country a few years earlier, I missed the closeness of my family, especially during those difficult times. They were pillars of strength from a distance, and their emotional and financial support were life-saving. But physically, I was on my own. Knowing my struggle, they offered to send us to family camp for a week during the summer. *Family camp?* I argued in my mind. *Are we even a family anymore?*

Bitterness had crept in, leaving me angry at God and myself. This was not how I dreamt my life would go, and it certainly wasn't the life I wanted for my girl. I reluctantly agreed to the summer camp offer, but I secretly wrestled with doubt that it would help us heal in any way.

Sometimes the things we least want to do are the pivot points that mean the most. Summer camp was like that for us. Arriving late with a wriggling toddler under one arm and a tattered diaper bag under the other, I felt very out of place in this family setting. We smelled like a combination of McDonalds french fries, dirty diapers, and the raspberry Jell-o® that had exploded in the backseat. Harnessing all the courage my twenty-five-year-old self could muster, I began to make my way to the bunk houses, trying to go unnoticed, certain this was a bad idea.

> Sometimes the things we least want to do are the pivot points that mean the most.

"Well, look at you two beauties," came an angelic voice from behind us. Lois danced her way toward us, eyes glittering with joy and a smile that felt like a hug. She was a welcome sight after our two-hour trip. In that moment, I felt at home with her. She goochy-gooed her way right into the heart of my toddler, and for the week of camp, she was God's perfectly placed messenger in my life.

For five days, Lois loved us well. She played with my little girl when I needed a break, and even when I didn't. She prayed beautiful prayers over us, sang Bible songs as she rocked my daughter to sleep, and listened while I shared the fears I held deep in my heart.

During our last campfire, while Lois held a sleeping toddler in her lap, she put her arm around my shoulder and said words I will never forget. "God is not punishing you, Nicole. He chose Delaney for you, knowing what you would go through. He knew she needed you to be her Mom. There are no mistakes here. Your little family of two is precious to Him."

Pivot.

Maybe this is obvious to you—it certainly wasn't to me. God chooses our kids for us. God chose Delaney for me. I was the right Mom for the job, and she was in good hands with me.

> Knowing what your family would go through, God decided you were the one He wanted to take care of His little ones.

And, my friend, you are the right Mom for the job too. Your children were chosen for you. Knowing what your family would go through, God decided you were the one He wanted to take care of His little ones.

What a compliment! And what a responsibility!

Returning home from camp that year started a new chapter in our lives. The situation was the same, but my view had changed. Perspective is everything. And when I agreed with God that He had made a good choice, that my little girl was in good hands with me, I started to move differently in my life.

God does not make mistakes, Mom. He has placed your little one in your home on purpose. The rejection you experienced and the changes in your family do not change His mind. Please think about this for a moment—you were chosen for your children, knowing what would happen. And God hasn't changed His mind about you.

Handpicked Partnership with the Creator of the Universe

Partnering with God is serious business. I remember sitting on the floor of our little basement suite, surrounded by boxes needing unpacking and overwhelmed with this new chapter. My exhausted little girl was asleep on the couch, wedged between a pile of stuffies and a box of bum wipes. Her favorite blanket was tucked up to her chin. *Toddlers are especially cute when they're asleep*, I thought to myself. And as I watched her, a powerful realization landed like thunder in my mind.

You must do this well.

I agreed. I needed to do this well, my daughter deserved that. But what did that even mean? How could I help my girl heal from our loss, navigate the changes, and move forward in a healthy way? And how could I help myself, as her Mom, provide a godly example of a woman of courage, faith, and hope?

In those early days, most of the people I knew had never been through a divorce or experienced the things we had gone through. Floundering in most areas of single parenting and helping my daughter through her grief, while still navigating my own, was a complex and messy battle. I wanted a checklist: *do this, don't do that.* And I longed to hear from someone who understood. In a parenting crisis, we need to hear from other moms who have travelled this painful road, about how they got through and how they helped their children manage.

If I could coach my twenty-five-year-old self through those difficult times, this is what I would tell her:

- "Your children will be okay, if you're okay. Moms set the tone for the home, and our children look to us to lead this trip through the valley. Believe me, I know you are not feeling equipped or even interested in leading this expedition, but you can do it. And you will look back on yourself with a smile, proud of what you accomplished. Your wellness is a necessity for your child's wellness. Take care of yourself, be active in your healing.

- "Name it and claim it. Helping our children learn to identify their emotions, giving them permission to feel the feels, is a gift that will last a lifetime. Put a feelings chart on the wall to help your child identify emotions, and then take opportunities throughout the day to practise expressing all of them. The good and not so good. Grief often shows up as anger, but at the bottom of the naughty behaviour or rage is a hurting heart that needs to be comforted and encouraged to grieve.

- "Resist the urge to *silver-line, ya-but,* or rush them through. When we paint a silver lining around the situation or "ya-but" things, we minimize our child's pain and communicate our own discomfort with emotions. It teaches our children to shut down and not share what they're feeling.
    - To silver line something looks like: 'At least you will get to see your Daddy this weekend.'
    - Ya-butting looks like: 'Yes, you don't live with Daddy right now, but you have several friends who don't live with their Daddy, and they are doing okay.'
- "Follow their lead. It doesn't always feel like the right time to have a deep conversation about feelings. And it doesn't always feel like the right time to call Daddy or Grandma. But when possible, make the time. Our child's timing is not at all connected to our timing, and when feelings come up it's a golden ticket into their hearts. This creates closeness and security.
- "Let your child love both of you. Loving her/his Daddy doesn't mean they don't love you. Encouraging a strong

bond is a gift to our kids, it helps them feel attached and safe. Torn children are wounded children.

- "Keep routine and relationships. The more healthy adults we have in the lives of our kids, the better. If visiting Grandma is a Wednesday thing, stick with it. The typical day-to-day activities that seem small to us are meaningful experiences with normalcy for our children. Routine allows for stability and feeds self-esteem and confidence.

- "If you can't say something nice or helpful for healing, don't say anything at all. You've been through a lot, and if I could guess, I'm sure there are plenty of choice words you have for your child's father. That's very normal, and I get it. Vent to your friend, talk to a therapist, yell it into your pillow, but don't diss your child's parent to them. It will feel good for a moment, but it hurts our kids and has lifelong implications.

- "Resist the urge to discuss details of your relationship and the reasons for separation. Sharing details, especially about what their father has done, is a real temptation for us women. But we must use extreme caution and decide not to disclose specifics to our children that will undermine healing or healthy relationships."

Through Their Little Eyes

Children experience changes in the family differently than we do. My personal and professional experience has shown me four distinct differences in how children process separation and major changes in their family dynamics:

1. Their loss is different. Children will feel abandoned too, but being left by a parent is very different from being abandoned by a spouse.

2. Their perspective is different. Children look up at the separation while we adults have an eye-to-eye view of it. This feels powerless, and in many cases children take on the responsibility of the relationship breakdown.

3. Their needs are different. These will vary depending on the developmental stage of your children, but it's safe to say that children are dependents, and they look to us to help them understand and navigate. They need security, reassurance, and stability, just like we do, but they are fully dependent on us to provide that for them.

4. Their emotion management skills are different. Again, depending on development, children will show emotions differently. In most cases they will either suppress them and try to show you they're okay, or enthusiastically express them, often in ways that look like anger, though they feel pain.

Dear friend, your children are looking to you for courage and stability. And while that is a heavy responsibility, and I know you are weary, you are absolutely the right person for this job. You will be okay and your children will be okay. Stay the course. Fix your eyes on Jesus and lean hard on Him as you hold these little ones He has entrusted to you. One day you will look back on this time of your life and understand all that God was up to. He has great plans for you and for your kids. He is trustworthy and He will never leave you or them.

KEY TAKEAWAYS

- Your children were chosen for you by God.

- Your situation is not a surprise to your Heavenly Father.

- He is passionately invested in your life.

- You are not being punished, you've not been forgotten, and you're not alone.

- Children grieve differently than adults.

- Creating space for your child to identify, understand, and communicate their feelings is a healthy way to help them grow.

- Conflict between parents leaves children feeling torn. This stunts healing.

- Grieving is essential, and making mistakes is okay.

REJECTION RECOVERY

Children are a gift from the LORD (Psalm 127:3a NLT).

THERAPEUTIC QUESTIONS

- What is it about being a mom that brings you joy?

- When you think about your identity as a mom, what strengths do you identify in yourself?

- What surprises you about motherhood? Why?

- What story would you like to tell about this time in your life? And what is the story you would like your children to tell about you?

JOURNAL PROMPT

This is a gratitude journal prompt.

These things made me laugh today   _____
_____

The beautiful things I noticed today are   _____
_____

My children leave me in awe when they do this   _____
_____

I am grateful for these ten things today   _____
_____
_____
_____

Thank you, Jesus, for my children. I am sometimes overwhelmed with the responsibility of caring for them while I also try to care for myself. I accept that you gave them to me and I am grateful that You trust me with them. Please equip me for this job, Lord. I want to do this well. Please protect them and hold them close to You, especially during these difficult days. You are a good Father and I trust You to lead us through this. Amen.

CHAPTER 20

Your Story
A Survival Guide for Another Woman's Soul

"Amazing things happen when women help other women."

—KASIA GOSPOS

Believe me when I tell you, your story is meant to be told. The bits and pieces that brought you to your knees are the building blocks to another woman's freedom.

Your hard-won-know-how and the lessons you've learned through your time in the valley will inform the healing of broken hearts. And, my friend, the journey you've taken will absolutely help others feel less alone in their own valley.

But know this for sure, while your rejection story is an important one, it's your journey to recovery that will bring healing to others.

> The bits and pieces that brought you to your knees are the building blocks to another woman's freedom.

Let's be honest, this has been hard. I know you've wondered why. Me too. So much of rejection doesn't make sense, and it reeks of injustice. I completely agree.

If we could sit together over coffee, we would talk about the wonderings. We would shake our heads at the awful and roll our eyes for the many times we felt lost in the valley.

And then we would tip our hat to rejection, collect our courage and remind ourselves that God's ways are higher. We would talk about what we've learned and about the pivot points full of hope and purpose. And we would look at each other in awe because we have been through the terrible and now hold a story of redemption.

> We have been through the terrible and now hold a story of redemption.

Pivots Away from Brokenness Toward Wholeness

Do you remember when I told you about the first day in my new church? My courage was in high gear that day as I approached that enormous building and made my way inside. When I reflect back on her, my younger self who carried shame and sorrow up that driveway and placed a nametag over her broken heart, I just want to high-five her. She did the hard thing, carried the heavy weight and followed her Heavenly Father's voice in the direction He was calling.

Let's not forget to remember these moments of courage-infused obedience in our younger selves. And let's not forget to remember the pivot points in our journey, when we listened hard to God's leading, allowing a shift in the movement through the valley.

Pivot points are powerful. They're the necessary components drawing us away from rejection, and they allow us to hear God when He calls us to share our valley to victory story.

My new church held all kinds of pivot points. Like the morning I swallowed my pride and walked to the front of the church for prayer, weeping openly as a woman half my age prayed for my broken marriage and my broken heart.

And then months later, the elderly woman who made her way across the sanctuary just to tell me that God had a plan for my sorrow and to trust Him with the healing.

The Caregroup members who embraced me with more love than I can humanly express, and the countless reminders in the open arms and bright smiles of the people in the pews around me. All big and small pivots.

Pivots away from broken, toward whole. Pivots away from shame, toward dignity. And pivots away from rejected, toward accepted. Let's keep our eyes open for God's hands, His voice in the people and places He has brought into our lives.

A Message I'll Never (Ever) Forget

Sunday after Sunday, the lead Pastors, Kim and Clark, delivered powerful messages of hope and healing. There were moments in each service where, if you had asked me, I was certain it was just me and those two power-preachers in the sanctuary. Their words were healing salve on my heart, as they declared me chosen by Jesus, anointed for His work, and purpose-driven. I tell you, I could literally feel the brokenness mend.

> Listen hard to the words spoken over you by godly, wise people. They will be the words of hope and healing you speak over others.

Listen hard to the words spoken over you by godly, wise people. They will be the words of hope and healing you speak over others.

Propped against the pulpit one Sunday, Kim held her Bible in the air and declared with conviction, "My job is to help make Jesus famous. And if my brokenness points people to Him, bring it on!"

Something happened inside me that day. You know those moments when everything else fades away, and it's just you and the moment locked in time? Kim's words grabbed me so tight, they took my breath away.

Amen! I said in my heart. *Amen.*

Pivot.

On that Sunday morning, I accepted the mission that had always been in front of me. The mission to use my story to help make Jesus famous.

I didn't like all the parts. Shame and anxiety still threatened to steer me off course. But if Jesus believed I could manage this story, I was going to choose to partner with Him and roll it out in a way that guides people in His direction.

This is about partnership with Jesus. And it's about partnership with others who are using their sorrow and pain to help make Jesus famous.

While we want to tuck the pain stories deep in the past, pretend they don't exist, and present to the world as people who have it all together, that doesn't serve Kingdom work.

> When we move from a mess-focused mentality to a ministry-minded perspective the curtain lifts.

When we move from a mess-focused mentality to a ministry-minded perspective the curtain lifts. Not only does our pain hold purpose, but God begins to bring hurting people into our lives who need to hear what we have learned in the valley. From this ministry-minded perspective we collect opportunities to share about the healing power of Jesus, planting us smack dab in the centre of someone else's pivot point.

Perspective is everything. If I look back on the valley of rejection as a desperate time of loss and allow the pain to inform my life, I will move through my days with an edge of resentment and suspicion. If I decide to hide or bury the brokenness and pretend I have lived a life free of sorrow, shame will follow me through my life, and the valley will have no purpose.

But when I embrace a ministry-mindset, and reflect back on the valley as field research, a rich learning opportunity to inform me and help others, it takes on new life. Suddenly, when I decide my wounds can help someone, the journey holds purpose. And through this lens, I am okay with the jagged road that informs my ministry.

> We must be good stewards of our story.

We must be good stewards of our story. When Kim challenged me from the pulpit to accept the mission God had given me and not to waste the pain, I made a decision. The last thing I want to do is stand before Jesus one day and have to explain why I didn't use every opportunity, every ounce of my messy life, to show people His love. His grace. His mercy.

> We are precious to Jesus.

Jesus - Our Ultimate Pivot Point

We are precious to Jesus. Messy lives, broken stories, sin and loss do not deter Him from His pursuit of His children. The countless women in the Bible whose lives were changed by Jesus are testament to His tender-hearted fondness for us.

I am fascinated by Mary Magdalene, a beloved friend and supporter of Jesus. How does a Jewish woman in need of an exorcism become one of Jesus' nearest and dearest? Battered and bruised, the Bible tells us she had been possessed by seven demons. Her emotional and physical suffering was tremendous, leaving her desperate for healing. Rejection was constant for her, and her life would have looked nothing like her childhood dreams. Mary Magdalene was living in a nightmare.

And then, Jesus arrived on the scene.

Jesus. He saw past the demons and peered into the eyes of a child He loved, a child He created. Recognizing His daughter, knowing her, He commanded the demons to leave. The gospels of Mark and Luke record the healing that took place in that pivotal moment for our dear sister. I can only imagine how she felt to be seen by Jesus, life spared, and freedom secured.

Wait. I *can* imagine, because, me too. I know what it's like to be seen, spared, and set free by Jesus. And, I imagine you do too.

Healed by Jesus as we know, becomes our new identity. And for our ancient sister, her gratitude prompted a life of servanthood, propelling her into a ministry mindset at the side of her Saviour. Like us, Mary Magdalene experienced both a rescue and a redemption when she accepted the life changing touch of Jesus. Released from her past, she was set free to be the woman God had created her to be.

And just like that, her new mission in life became serving alongside Jesus. The past was behind her, and the awfulness of her history did not keep her from being an active messenger of the Good news. In fact, it's her story that promotes healing for women like me.

I need to know about the Mary Magdalenes of the past whose brokenness did not render her unworthy to do important ministry. I need reminding, through these historical people, that Jesus meets us in our valley. He remains unphased by our mess and points a loving finger in our direction, saying, "My precious child, come with me, I have important work for you to do."

Redeemed by Jesus, Mary walked closely with her Saviour. She watched Him live and minister, and then Mary Magdalene watched her Saviour die. She was there when He was taken off the cross, and with heartache and sorrow, she made her way into the garden where He was buried.

Everything slows down for me as I reflect on the next part of Mary's story. It was Sunday morning, and Mary went to the tomb where she had watched Jesus's body placed just days earlier. To her horror, the stone had been rolled away. She runs, frenzied, to recruit some of the disciples, hurrying them to the scene.

Note what happens next. The disciples, after examining the empty tomb, return to their homes, leaving Mary alone in the garden, grieving her Saviour. We know she is weeping, as she musters the courage to peek inside the tomb to see for herself. Her longing to be close to Jesus drives her to look, and what she finds changes everything. John 20:12 says Mary sees *"two angels in white, seated where Jesus's body had been, one at the head and the other at the foot."*

Mary explains to the angels why she is crying, *"They have taken my Lord away,"* she said, *"And I don't know where they have put Him"*

(John 20:13b). Confused and heartbroken, our sweet sister turns around and finds Jesus, whom she thinks is a gardener, standing close by.

He asks her, *"Woman, why are you crying? Who is it you are looking for?"* (John 20:15a).

In her desperation, Mary blurts out, *"Sir, if you have carried him away, tell me where you have put him, and I will get him"* (John 20:15b).

And then, dripping with tenderness and love, Jesus simply says, *"Mary"* (John 20:16b).

Pivot.

Can you just imagine this scene? Mary, frantic and broken, grieving the One she loved, confused, but determined to find her Lord, stands in the presence of her Risen Saviour. He had been dead, and now He was alive. An overflowing to-do list did not deter Him—Jesus made time to meet with Mary.

My heart is racing as I write this. I just want to yell out, "Jesus! You are so cool! Thank You for waiting for Mary that day. Thank You for loving her enough to show us through this moment how precious Your children are to You."

But let's not miss the next important part of Mary's story—she is tasked with a mission.

Pivot again.

Mary had a job to do. Jesus wanted her to go and tell the disciples what she knew. He tasked a woman, a formerly demon-possessed and outcast woman, with the job of declaring His resurrection. I get goosebumps when I think of the awesomeness of this.

Three distinctly incredible things happened for Mary that day:

1. Jesus waited for her—communicating *I love you*.
2. Jesus called her by name—communicating *I know you*.
3. Jesus tasked her with a mission—communicating *I trust you with my message*.

We are Mary Magdalenes too, you and me. Broken from the injuries of the past but repurposed to help make Jesus famous. He has entrusted us with a message to speak into the lives of others, and with this divine appointment comes significant responsibility.

If I'm honest, it's easier for me to cling to Jesus in the valley than in the victory. My face plants usually drive me to His feet in desperation. Perhaps that's why He's allowed me a few doozies. The valley is God's training ground, rich with teaching and full of growth. But when He accompanies us out to the other side, that's when we get to partner with Him.

The valley promotes dependency on God, and it's where we learn of His love and His power to heal. The valley is about us. It's the place God moves in, picks us up, and repairs our brokenness. But on the other side of the valley, when we stop for a moment to enjoy the fresh air of healing, we are handed our mission. Because the other side of the valley is about others. And without exception, our job is to show people the unshakeable, relentless love of Jesus through our testimony of healing.

To be effective in this mission, we must stay close to our Leader. We are anointed and appointed with a unique valley to victory story. And as we move forward we must keep our eyes locked on Him, in line with His plan, and available for His work.

He brought us through the terrible, taught us the truth, and is tasking us with the tremendous. What an opportunity to partner together to help make Jesus famous.

KEY TAKEAWAYS

- Our valley to victory story is someone else's guidebook to healing.

- Being ministry-minded opens up opportunities to be part of another woman's pivot points.

- Collect pivot points in the valley, they will help you speak encouragement to others.

- Jesus waits for us. He knows our name, and He has a ministry for us.

- The message of your recovery is your ministry.

- Stay focused on Jesus.

REJECTION RECOVERY

God did this so that they would seek him and perhaps reach out for Him and find him, though he is not far from any one of us (Acts 17:27).

THERAPEUTIC ACTIVITY

- Write a letter to your younger self. Point out pivot points, remind that younger you of hope, and tell her about your life now.

- Spend some time in the silence of your heart, Bible and journal open. Ask Jesus how you can help make Him famous. Write out what comes to your mind.

JOURNAL PROMPT

How will you use this hard-won-know-how to help others? What is the story you want to share about healing?

Dear Jesus, I want to help make you famous. You have rescued me from a devastating season of my life and while there are still pain points and heartache, healing is happening. I know You have a plan. I want to stay close to You, and partner with You in reaching hurting hearts. Please give me opportunities to minister to people. Please help me use my story with wisdom and purpose, always giving you the glory for what You have done and are doing in my life. I love you Jesus. Amen.

Some Final Thoughts

"The place where you are right now, God circled on a map for you."

—Hafiz

Facing the awful has required a lot from us. We've harnessed our courage, locked eyes with Hope, and put one weary foot in front of the other.

And, here we are.

If we could only honour this victory in person together, what a celebration that would be! I would hug you, high-five you, and nod my head emphatically. It would be a knowing nod to tell you, *I knew you could do it.*

Well done, you.

Our field research has been intense, hasn't it? The bumps and bruises remind us that the journey to healing is not for the faint of heart. It's a knock-down-drag-out battle of the wills, and a daily decision to pick up a heavy dose of determination, harnessing courage to walk another day toward victory.

> Recovery is a process. A process of trust and faith in the One Who created us, a process of renewal, as we cling to Him continually, even on this side of things.

Recovery is a process. A process of trust and faith in the One Who created us, a process of renewal, as we cling to Him continually, even on this side of things.

This used to be hard to understand for me, but we serve a God Who allows pain. He allows rejection, injustice, and loss.

The story He has allowed, dare I say chosen, for my life is not necessarily one I would have signed up for. But in every way, He is right.

He equips us for what He calls us to.

Endings make way for the new. As I write this, snow is piling up on the windowsill of my office. The office in my new house, in the new life I share with my new husband, Brent. I am home.

I wish I could tell you all the details of this homecoming. But from this view, I can see the bigger picture. I may not fully understand why God allowed the pain—or why He allowed the trauma of rejection. But I see where He was taking me and who He was making me.

And now, I understand that I am wanted.

Being rejected into the arms of Love taught me to see myself through my Father's eyes. I am not what has been said of me. And my worth and lovability is not connected to my marital status, who wants me, or what has happened.

The beautiful gift of being loved by Brent is not lost on me. But it doesn't define me. My identity is in Jesus. Because He wants me—because He says I am chosen and loved—I am free.

My friend, I don't know what awesome pivot points are ahead for you. I don't know what God is going to do in your life that will leave you in awe of His kindness and love. But I do know it's coming. I do know He promises to make beautiful things from broken places. And I do know that when He has taught you what He needs you to know, He will create incredible opportunities for you to tell others about His goodness.

You are loved. And you are desperately wanted and wholeheartedly chosen by the King of Kings.

It is my prayer that you not only accept your new identity, but that you step into your life, owning every ounce of it.

Thank you, my friend, for the incredible privilege of journeying with you through your valley. And thank you for travelling with me through the writing of this book. It has been an important part of my healing and a journey I will never forget.

With love,
Nicole

SCRIPTURES TO

Ease Anxiety and Bring Comfort

Isaiah 41:10: *"Don't be afraid, for I am with you. Don't be discouraged, for I am your God. I will strengthen you and help you. I will hold you up with my victorious right hand"* (NLT).

Psalm 34:4–5: *"I sought the Lord, and he answered me and delivered me from all my fears. Those who look to him are radiant, and their faces shall never be ashamed"* (ESV).

2 Timothy 1:7: *"For God gave us a spirit not of fear but of power and love and self-control"* (ESV).

Psalm 34:17–18: *"The LORD hears his people when they call to him for help. He rescues them from all their troubles. The LORD is close to the brokenhearted; he rescues those whose spirits are crushed"* (NLT).

Isaiah 35:4: *"Say to those who have an anxious heart, "Be strong, fear not! Behold, your God will come with vengeance, with the recompense of God. He will come and save you"* (ESV).

Isaiah 40:31: *"But they who wait for the LORD shall renew their strength: they shall mount up with wings like eagles; they shall run and not be weary; they shall walk and not faint"* (ESV).

Hebrews 11:1: *"Now faith is the assurance of things hoped for, the conviction of things not seen"* (ESV).

John 14:1: *"Don't let your hearts be troubled. Trust in God, and trust also in me"* (NLT).

James 1:2–3: "*Count it all joy, my brothers, when you meet trials of various kinds, for you know that the testing of your faith produces steadfastness*" (ESV).

Luke 12:22- 25: "*And he said to his disciples, "Therefore I tell you, do not be anxious about your life, what you will eat, nor about your body, what you will put on. For life is more than food, and the body more than clothing. Consider the ravens: they neither sow nor reap, they have neither storehouse nor barn, and yet God feeds them. Of how much more value are you than the birds! And which of you by being anxious can add a single hour to his span of life?*" (ESV).

Psalm 138:8: "*The Lord will fulfill his purpose for me; your steadfast love, O LORD, endures forever. Do not forsake the work of your hands*" (ESV).

Roman 8:38–39: "*For I am sure that neither death nor life, nor angels nor rulers, nor things present nor things to come, nor powers, nor height nor depth, nor anything else in all creation, will be able to separate us from the love of God in Christ Jesus our LORD*" (ESV).

Jeremiah 29:11: "*For I know the plans I have for you, declares the LORD, plans for welfare and not for evil, to give you a future and a hope*" (ESV).

Jeremiah 17:7–8: "*Blessed is the man who trusts in the LORD, whose trust is in the LORD. He is like a tree planted by water, that sends out its roots by the stream, and does not fear when heat comes, for its leaves remain green, and is not anxious in the year of drought, for it does not cease to bear fruit*" (ESV).

Philippians 4:6–7: "*do not be anxious about anything, but in everything by prayer and supplication with thanksgiving let your requests be made known to God. And the peace of God, which surpasses all understanding, will guard your hearts and your minds in Christ Jesus"* (ESV).

Matthew 11:28–30: *"Then Jesus said, 'Come to me, all of you who are weary and carry heavy burdens, and I will give you rest"* (NLT).

John 14:27: *"Peace I leave with you; my peace I give to you. Not as the world gives do I give to you. Let not your hearts be troubled, neither let them be afraid"* (ESV).

Psalm 55:22: *"Cast your burden on the LORD, and he will sustain you; he will never permit the righteous to be moved"* (ESV).

Zephaniah 3:17: *"The LORD your God is in your midst, a mighty one who will save; he will rejoice over you with gladness; he will quiet you by his love; he will exult over you with loud singing"* (ESV).

Romans 10:13: *"For everyone who calls on the name of the Lord will be saved"* (ESV).

Psalm 71:20–21: *"You who have made me see many troubles and calamities will revive me again; from the depths of the earth you will bring me up again. You will increase my greatness and comfort me again"* (ESV).

John 1:5: *"The light shines in the darkness, and the darkness has not overcome it"* (ESV).

Philippians 1:6: *"Being confident of this, that he who began a good work in you will carry it on to completion until the day of Christ Jesus."*

Joshua 1:9: *"Have I not commanded you? Be strong and courageous. Do not be frightened, and do not be dismayed, for the Lord your God is with you wherever you go"* (ESV).

Acknowledgments

I am loved by Jesus—it's a truth that continues to amaze me. And while I see His fingerprints all over my life, the most beautiful evidence of His love is the steadfast presence of the incredible people He has given me.

Brent: You have my heart. Thank you for your courageous love, unconditional acceptance, and unceasing support. I am a better woman because of you. This book was hard to write, and I imagine it's been even harder for you to read. Thank you for leaning into the *hard* with me and for being my partner and best friend. We are at the beginning of a beautiful chapter together. And there's no one I'd rather write it with than you. I love you.

Delaney: My beautiful, brave girl. Your courage to travel the tough spots, and your remarkable bounce-back inspires me. I have loved watching you grow, and am so grateful God allowed me to be your mom. Thank you for teaching me about unconditional love. And thank you for being my side-kick through the last twenty-five years. I have learned so much from you. And I am very proud of you. You are my sunshine—I love you to the moon and back.

Mom and Dad: The people who pointed me toward Jesus as a child and have continued to hold me up to Him through every valley, and every victory. You simply are the best! No one has held on tighter to me than you two. Thank you for believing in me and helping me use my story. I can never thank you enough.

Paul: There is no better brother for me. I am so grateful for your friendship and love. Thank you for standing with me and being the gentle voice of reason when things did not at all feel okay. And thank you for cheering me on through the valley and into the writing of this book. P.S: I accept blame for the bow and arrow situation, but I did not push you out of the treehouse. Tell the kids.

Jackie: Your editing expertise amazes me. I cannot thank you enough for the countless hours you committed to chasing commas.

My valley to victory cheerleaders: Corina, Debbie, Diane, Jen, Karen: You are THE best! In so many ways you have been God's hands in my life—encouraging me, loving me, and reminding me of the Truth. Your love has been exactly what I needed when I felt weary or ill-equipped to write this book. God has blessed me so much through our friendship.

Robyn, Anita, and the rest of the team at Brookstone Creative Group: Your direction, encouragement, wisdom, and expertise has meant the message on my heart finally found its way. Thank you.

The women mentioned in this book: Thank you for allowing me the privilege of being part of your story. Your courage impacted my life, and now it is my heart's desire that others will also learn from you as well. You are braver than you know.

To you, the woman reading these words: I have so many things I want to say to you. I wish we could do this in person. But please know you have travelled with me through the writing of every word. I believe in you, and I think you're remarkable.

Jesus: You never cease to amaze me! What would I do without you? Where would I be? It's all for you. Thank you for those days in the valley and for those times you carried me. And thank you for trusting me with this story. I humbly offer it back to you. Your love, Your grace, and Your kindness take my breath away. Thank you.

ABOUT THE AUTHOR

Nicole Langman

Nicole had no plans of writing about rejection recovery—until she found herself face down in her own field research wrestling with her new reality. This struggle was more like an emotional barroom brawl than anything else. It was in the mess Nicole finally found her true identity—Wanted by the King of Kings. Chosen by Jesus. Adored.

With the blindside of an ended marriage in the rearview mirror, Nicole set out to remind others of their worth. She is passionate about encouraging women to reclaim the truth of who they are, and leave behind the mental chatter, hurtful messages, and painful pasts holding them hostage.

She writes from her home in rural Ontario, close to the shores of Georgian Bay. She is newly married to Brent, a reality that leaves her in awe of God's goodness. He really does bring beauty from ashes! Together they are navigating a new life with three adult children and a wacky Bernedoodle named Sadie.

Nicole's personal field research in the valley of rejection has inspired this book and her ebook: *Rejection Recovery Resource Kit*.

Connect with the Author

Nicole would love to connect with you. You can find her at:

Website: www.nicolelangman.com

Facebook: https:/facebook.com/nicolelangmanofficialpage

Instagram: www.instagram.com/nicole_langman_officialprofile

If you are interested in having Nicole speak at your event, please email her at nicole@nicolelangman.com

Notes

CHAPTER 3
1 Brown, B. (2014), Shame vs Guilt, www.brenebrowncom/blog/2013
2 Office of the Surgeon General (US); National Centre for Injury Prevention and Control (US).; National Institute of Mental Health (US); Centre for Mental Health Services (US); Youth Violence: A report of the Surgeon General. Rockville (MD); Office of the Surgeon General (US); 2001. PMD: 20669522

CHAPTER 6
3 Mirriam-Webster Dictionary, s.v. "relished". https://www.mirriam-webster.com/dictionary/relished

CHAPTER 8
4 Lewis, C.S, Mere Christianity (New York: HarperOne, 2001)

CHAPTER 13
5 Mirraim-Webster Dictionary, s.v. "courage" https://www.mirriam-webster.com/dictionary/courage
6 Brown, B. Rising Strong (2015)

CHAPTER 14
7 Song by Angela Turner - Daughter of the Daylight (2011)

CHAPTER 15
8 TerKeurst, L. (2018), It's Not Supposed to Be This Way.

CHAPTER 17
9 Ponder, C. (1988), The Dynamic Law of Prosperity
10 TerKeurst, L. (2020). Forgiving What You Can't Forget.

CHAPTER 18
11 Grief Recovery Institute. www.greifrecovermethod.com/blog/2013/07/grief-why-comparing-losses-never-helps-and-often-hurts.

Made in the USA
Middletown, DE
06 January 2025

68912770R00163